ANIMALS

McGRAW-HILL

SCIENCE

MACMILLAN/McGRAW-HILL EDITION

ANIMALS

RICHARD MOYER ■ **LUCY DANIEL** ■ **JAY HACKETT**
PRENTICE BAPTISTE ■ **PAMELA STRYKER** ■ **JOANNE VASQUEZ**

NATIONAL
GEOGRAPHIC
SOCIETY

McGraw-Hill School Division

New York   Farmington

PROGRAM AUTHORS

Dr. Lucy H. Daniel
*Teacher, Consultant
Rutherford County Schools,
North Carolina*

Dr. Jay Hackett
*Emeritus Professor of Earth
Sciences
University of Northern
Colorado*

Dr. Richard H. Moyer
*Professor of Science
Education
University of Michigan-
Dearborn*

Dr. H. Prentice Baptiste
*Professor of Curriculum and
Instruction
New Mexico State
University*

Pamela Stryker, M.Ed.
*Elementary Educator and
Science Consultant
Eanes Independent School
District
Austin, Texas*

JoAnne Vasquez, M.Ed.
*Elementary Science
Education Specialist
Mesa Public Schools,
Arizona
NSTA President 1996–1997*

NATIONAL
GEOGRAPHIC
SOCIETY

Washington, D.C.

CONTRIBUTING AUTHORS

Dr. Thomas Custer
Dr. James Flood
Dr. Diane Lapp
Doug Llewellyn
Dorothy Reid
Dr. Donald M. Silver

CONSULTANTS

Dr. Danny J. Ballard
Dr. Carol Baskin
Dr. Bonnie Buratti
Dr. Suellen Cabe
Dr. Shawn Carlson
Dr. Thomas A. Davies
Dr. Marie DiBerardino
Dr. R. E. Duhrkopf
Dr. Ed Geary
Dr. Susan C. Giarratano-Russell
Dr. Karen Kwitter
Dr. Donna Lloyd-Kolkin
Ericka Lochner, RN
Donna Harrell Lubcker
Dr. Dennis L. Nelson
Dr. Fred S. Sack
Dr. Martin VanDyke
Dr. E. Peter Volpe
Dr. Josephine Davis Wallace
Dr. Joe Yelderman

Invitation to Science, *World of Science*, and *FUNtastic Facts* features found in this textbook were designed and developed by the National Geographic Society's Education Division.
Copyright © 2000 National Geographic Society
The name "National Geographic Society" and the Yellow Border Rectangle are trademarks of the Society, and their use, without prior written permission, is strictly prohibited.

Cover Photo: *bkgnd.* Art Wolfe/Tony Stone Images; *inset* Art Wolfe/Tony Stone Images

McGraw-Hill School Division

A Division of The McGraw·Hill Companies

McGraw-Hill School Division
Two Penn Plaza
New York, New York 10121

Printed in the United States of America

ISBN 0-02-278218-4 / 4

2 3 4 5 6 7 8 9 071/046 05 04 03 02 01 00

CONTENTS

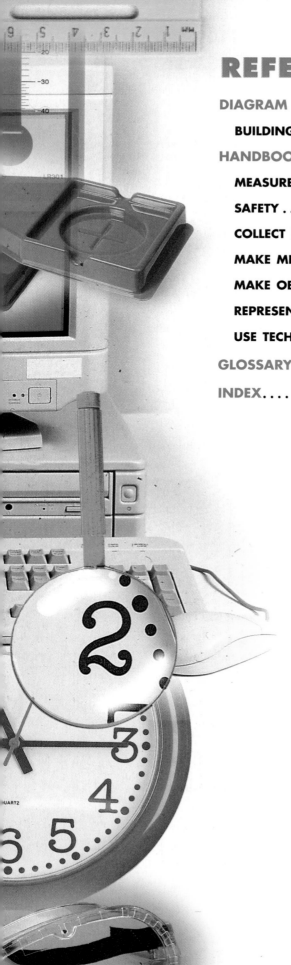

REFERENCE SECTION

CHAPTER 7
DESCRIBING ANIMALS

In this chapter you will learn about the characteristics of animals. You will also learn about the two large groups into which all animals are classified. When you are done studying this chapter, you will be able to classify all the pets you know!

In this chapter you will have many opportunities to represent information in an outline. An outline describes a subject, its main ideas, and its supporting details.

WHY IT MATTERS

Sometimes it is not easy to tell whether or not an organism is an animal.

SCIENCE WORDS

food chain shows the steps in which organisms get the food they need to survive

food web shows how food chains in an ecosystem are related

vertebrate an animal with a backbone

invertebrate an animal without a backbone

symmetry the way an animal's body parts match up around a point or central line

sponge the simplest kind of invertebrate

Animal Characteristics

How would you describe an animal? Think about any animals you know. Don't forget that you are an animal, too. What types of characteristics, or traits, do animals have in common?

EXPLORE

HYPOTHESIZE Animals come in many sizes and shapes, yet they all have certain characteristics. For example, what are the main characteristics of a fish and snail? Write a hypothesis in your *Science Journal.* How could you test your ideas?

EXPLORE ACTIVITY

Investigate the Characteristics of Animals

Observe the characteristics of a snail and a fish to compare how they are similar and different.

MATERIALS

- clear container with aquarium water
- water snail
- goldfish or guppy
- fish food
- ruler
- *Science Journal*

PROCEDURES

Safety: Be careful with live animals.

1. Obtain a beaker with a fish and a snail in it.

2. **OBSERVE** Record the shape and approximate size of both animals in your *Science Journal*. Describe how each animal moves and any other observations that you make.

3. **OBSERVE** Add a few flakes of fish food to the beaker. What do the animals do? Record your observations.

4. **DRAW CONCLUSIONS** What does the fish eat? The snail?

CONCLUDE AND APPLY

1. **IDENTIFY** What body parts does each animal have? How do they use these parts?

2. **COMPARE** Compare how the fish and the snail move. Is movement an advantage for the animals? Explain.

3. **INFER** Do you think the fish and the snail are made of one cell or many cells? Why?

4. **IDENTIFY** What characteristics do the fish and the snail have? Make a list. Compare your list with other groups' lists. Make a class list.

GOING FURTHER: Apply

5. **COMPARE** How are you similar to the fish and the snail? How are you different?

What Are the Characteristics of Animals?

The Explore Activity showed some of the characteristics that all animals have in common.

1. Animals are made of many cells.

• Each cell has a nucleus and a cell membrane.

• Animal cells do not have a cell wall or chlorophyll, like plants.

• Different cells have different jobs. Bone cells support and protect. Nerve cells carry messages.

2. Animals reproduce.

• Some animals have thousands of offspring, or young, in their lifetimes. Others have only a few.

• Many animals care for and protect their offspring.

3. Animals move in some way.

• Most animals move during some time of their life.

• Animals move by walking, running, flying, gliding, crawling, and swimming.

• Animals move to find food, escape danger, find mates, and find a new home.

4. Animals grow and change.

• Some animals change form as they grow.

• Some animals just grow larger.

5. Animals eat food.

• Animals cannot make their own food, like plants.

• They get food by eating plants or other animals.

• Animals digest food for energy.

• Animals use oxygen to turn their food into energy.

Some animals change form as they grow older. This moth began its life as a caterpillar.

How Do Organisms Get Energy?

All living things need energy to stay alive. Animals get energy from food. A food chain (füd chān) tells you the steps of how energy flows among a group of organisms. An ecosystem can have many different food chains. Combined they form a food web (füd web). A food web shows how food chains in an ecosystem are related.

A FOOD CHAIN

1 Energy comes from the Sun.

5 After organisms die, decomposers like fungi and bacteria break down their remains into chemicals.

2 Producers use it to make food.

6 Now all the energy in the food chain has been converted to heat. The chemicals are absorbed into the soil. They are used by producers as nutrients to make more food, along with energy from the Sun. The cycle starts again.

3 Consumers that eat the plants are primary consumers. They use some of the energy to maintain life functions. The rest is lost as heat.

4 Secondary consumers get energy by eating other consumers.

READING 🔥 DIAGRAMS

REPRESENT Draw and label another food chain.

213

How Are Animals Different?

All animals have the same things in common. They all have five basic characteristics—they are made of cells, they reproduce, they move in some way, they grow and change, and they eat food.

However, animals are also different in many ways. One major difference is having or not having a backbone. An animal with a backbone is called a **vertebrate** (vûr′tə brāt′). An animal without a backbone is called an **invertebrate** (in vûr′tə brit). You will learn more about vertebrates and invertebrates later in this chapter.

Brain Power

Which animal in the Explore Activity was a vertebrate? Which one was an invertebrate?

How Body Plans Differ

Another difference among animals is the way their body parts match up around a point or central line. This is known as **symmetry** (sim′ə trē). Body parts with symmetry match up as mirror images when they are folded over.

Some animals have no symmetry. One example is a **sponge** (spunj), the simplest kind of invertebrate. No matter how you fold a sponge, its body parts do not match up.

A sponge has no symmetry.

An animal with *radial* (rā′dē əl) symmetry has body parts that extend outward from a central point. You could fold a sea star through its center five ways and it would match up.

An animal with a sphere-shaped body, like a sea urchin, has *spherical* (sfer′i kəl) symmetry. You could fold a sea urchin any way through its center and it would match up.

An animal with *bilateral* (bī lat′ər əl) symmetry has only two sides, which are mirror images. You could fold a butterfly only one way through its center to have it match up. Organisms with bilateral symmetry have a definite front end, back end, upper side, and lower side. Invertebrates most commonly have radial and bilateral symmetry.

TYPES OF SYMMETRY

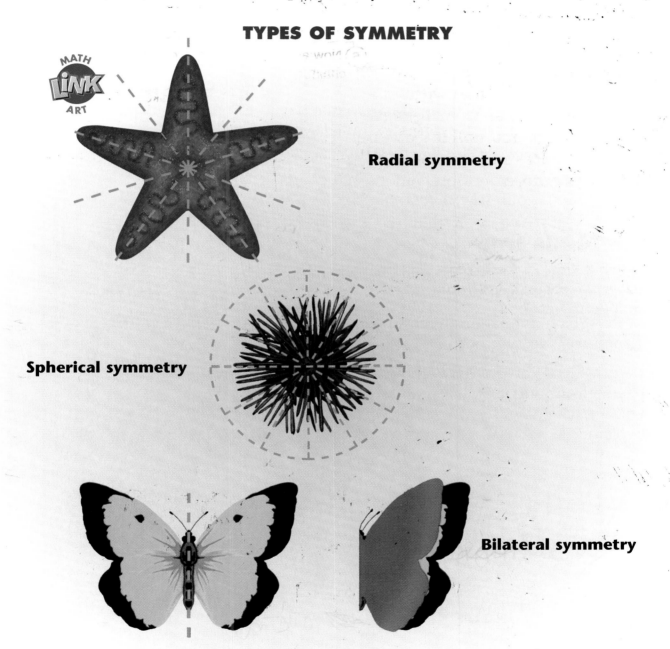

Radial symmetry

Spherical symmetry

Bilateral symmetry

Skill: Observing

ANIMAL SYMMETRY

A scientist's most important job is to *observe*, or look closely at, things. When you observe carefully, you often see things that you didn't know were there. You can practice your observation skills by looking for symmetry in different animals.

PROCEDURES

1. **IDENTIFY** Determine whether each animal has no symmetry, spherical symmetry, radial symmetry, or bilateral symmetry.

2. **CLASSIFY** Record your observations in a chart you create in your *Science Journal*.

CONCLUDE AND APPLY

1. **IDENTIFY** Which animal or animals have radial symmetry? Bilateral symmetry?

2. **INFER** Which animal or animals have spherical symmetry? No symmetry?

3. **EXPLAIN** Does an animal with radial symmetry have a front end and a back end? Explain.

FUNtastic Facts

It looks like a cross between a horse and a salad, but it's a fish. This foot-long animal—the leafy sea dragon—lives off the coast of Australia. Its wavy spines and leaflike appearance help conceal it on the seabed where it feeds. How might the fish's appearance help it survive?

WHY IT MATTERS

Before you can learn about the different animals with which you share the world, you need to know how to identify an animal. Sometimes you can be confused or even fooled. Look at the organism in the picture. Do you think it is a plant or an animal? What characteristics would you look for to identify it as an animal?

Is this a plant or an animal? How could you find out?

REVIEW

1. What characteristics do all animals have?

2. What is the difference between a vertebrate and an invertebrate?

3. How is radial symmetry different from bilateral symmetry?

4. **OBSERVE** What kind of symmetry does your own body have? Draw a diagram that shows how you could fold your body so each half matched up.

5. **CRITICAL THINKING** *Analyze* What do you think would happen if one organism was removed from a food chain?

WHY IT MATTERS THINK ABOUT IT
How do you know that you are an animal?

WHY IT MATTERS WRITE ABOUT IT
What if you discovered a new organism? How would you test to see if it was an animal? Describe some observations and tests you would do.

Once in the Wild

Drawing of aurochs
on cave wall

History of Science

Mouflon

Did you know that the kinds of animals people have as pets were once wild? So were the kinds of animals now raised on farms.

Thousands of years ago, people began domesticating wild animals, or adapting them to live with and around humans. Over time, the animals began to look and act different from their wild ancestors.

Wolves

The ancestor of the dog is the wolf. Wolves probably hung around ancient people to get leftover scraps of meat. Wolves lived and hunted in packs. Training them to live and hunt with humans was a natural development.

Ancient people hunted the cow's ancestor, the dangerous aurochs. They drew it on cave walls. Over time, people began keeping and raising cattle. They bred some cows to give milk and others to produce meat.

The mouflon is the sheep's ancestor. It still lives in parts of Europe and Asia. Before there were farms, humans gathered wool from wild sheep. Then people learned to raise sheep for wool. Trained dogs may have helped people round up the sheep.

Discussion Starter

1 Why did people domesticate some animals?

2 How did domesticating wolves help people? How did it help wolves?

*inter*NET CONNECTION To learn more about domesticated animals, visit www.mhschool.com/science and enter the keyword **DOMESTIC.**

WHY IT MATTERS

Many interesting animals do not have a backbone.

SCIENCE WORDS

cnidarian an invertebrate with poison stingers on tentacles

mollusk a soft-bodied invertebrate

echinoderm a spiny-skinned invertebrate

endoskeleton an internal supporting structure

arthropod an invertebrate with jointed legs and a body that is divided into sections

exoskeleton a hard covering that protects an invertebrate's body

Animals Without Backbones

Have you ever seen an organism like this? What do you think it is?

In 1909 Charles Walcott, an American scientist, found an interesting rock. It contained more than 100 fossils of animals that lived about 530 million years ago! Some animals were very strange. One, like the fossil and model below, show five eyes. Another was so strange that scientists couldn't tell if it was right-side up or upside down!

EXPLORE

HYPOTHESIZE Many of Walcott's fossils were invertebrates. What characteristics do you think invertebrates have? Write a hypothesis in your *Science Journal*. How could you test your ideas?

Investigate the Characteristics of Invertebrates

Observe some invertebrates to find out what common characteristics they have.

MATERIALS

- living planarian
- living earthworm
- hand lens
- petri dish
- water
- damp paper towel
- toothpick
- *Science Journal*

PROCEDURES

Safety: Be careful with live animals.

1. **OBSERVE** Place the worm on the damp paper towel. Get a petri dish with a planarian (plə nâr′ē ən) in it from your teacher. Observe each organism with a hand lens. Record your observations in your *Science Journal*.

2. **OBSERVE** Gently touch the worm with your finger and the planarian with the toothpick. What do they do? Record your observations in your *Science Journal*.

3. **OBSERVE** What characteristics of the praying mantis and magnified hydra do you observe? Record your observations.

CONCLUDE AND APPLY

1. **DRAW CONCLUSIONS** What characteristics do you think invertebrates have? Make a list.

2. **COMPARE AND CONTRAST** Compare your list with those of other classmates. Based on your observations, make a class list of invertebrate characteristics.

3. **COMPARE AND CONTRAST** How are Walcott's ancient invertebrates like invertebrates that live today? Do they have similar characteristics? How are they different?

GOING FURTHER: Apply

4. **IDENTIFY** Think of other organisms that you would classify as invertebrates based on your observations. Make a list. Check your list as you continue this topic.

What Are the Characteristics of Invertebrates?

As the Explore Activity showed, invertebrates come in a variety of shapes and sizes. The one thing that they have in common is the one thing that they lack—a backbone.

Classifying Invertebrates

How many different types of animals do you think there are in the world? Would you believe more than one million? Keeping track of them must be a BIG JOB! The first step is to classify them into groups. Animals can be classified into two large groups—vertebrates and invertebrates.

Nearly 95 out of every 100 animals are invertebrates. Invertebrates are divided into smaller groups based on their characteristics. Each group is called a *phylum* (fī′ləm). You will learn about eight invertebrate phyla in this lesson. *Phyla* is the plural of *phylum*.

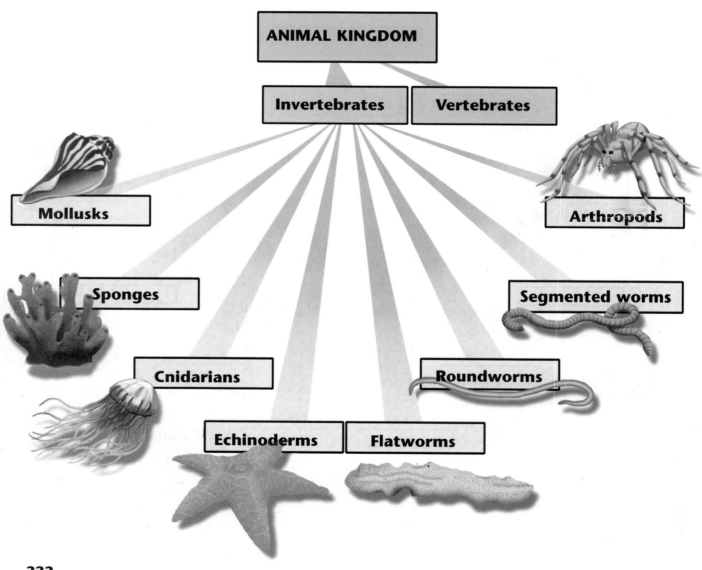

ANIMAL KINGDOM

Invertebrates

Vertebrates

Mollusks

Arthropods

Sponges

Segmented worms

Cnidarians

Roundworms

Echinoderms

Flatworms

Slime on the clown fish's body protects it from the sea anemone's stingers.

Some natural sponges are collected, dried, and sold for household use.

How Simple Is Simple?

Sponges

Sponges are the simplest invertebrates. You've already seen some sponges on page 214. A sponge's body is shaped like a sack, with an opening at the top. A sponge's body has no symmetry, is hollow, and does not have bones. A sponge's body is made of two cell layers with a jelly-like substance between the layers.

Water and food flow into the sponge through holes in its body. Water and wastes move out through the opening at the top.

A young sponge moves about until it finds a place to settle. An adult doesn't move from place to place. It filters the water passing through its body, eating bacteria, single-celled algae, and protists. A sponge can also grow back a missing part.

Cnidarians

Imagine an animal that shoots poison darts at its enemies! **Cnidarians** (nī dâr'ē ənz) are invertebrates that use poison stingers on tentacles to capture prey and for protection. Cnidarians, like sponges, have bodies that are two cell layers thick. However, they are more complex than sponges. Cnidarians have simple tissues and a mouth. They also have radial symmetry.

There are three major cnidarian groups, or classes. The hydra in the Explore Activity is one example. A hydra has a tube-shaped body and lives anchored to a surface. A jellyfish has a body shaped like an umbrella and floats freely in the water. Sea anemones and corals make up the third group. Groups of coral form coral reefs.

How Are Worms Classified?

Flatworms

Worms are classified into several phyla. You will learn about three phyla.

The planaria in the Explore Activity is a type of flatworm. Flatworms are more complex than cnidarians or sponges, but they are the simplest worms. They have flat, ribbonlike bodies with a head and a tail. Their bodies have bilateral symmetry and are three cell layers thick.

One group of flatworms includes the planaria. They live in fresh water and eat food with a mouth. Undigested food and wastes pass out through the mouth, too. Another group includes parasites. They have no mouth or digestive system, and live and feed inside the bodies of other animals. They absorb digested food in the host's intestines.

A tapeworm is a parasite that can live in many host animals, including people!

An adult roundworm *Ascaris* can grow to 40 centimeters (16 inches) long. It can also lay up to 200,000 eggs a day!

Roundworms

Roundworms have a slender, rounded body with pointed ends. The *Ascaris* (as′kə rəs), hookworm, and vinegar eel are typical roundworms. Some roundworms, like the *Ascaris* and hookworm, are parasites. They cause illness in people and other animals. About 2,500 species of roundworms are parasites of plants and animals. Others, like the vinegar eel, do not depend on one particular organism for food or a place to live. They can live on land and in water.

Roundworms are more complex than flatworms. They have a one-way digestive system. In a one-way system, food comes into the body through one opening. Waste leaves through another opening at the opposite end of the animal's body.

Segmented Worms

Have you ever seen or touched an earthworm? Earthworms, sandworms, and leeches are in the phylum of segmented worms.

Segmented worms have bodies that are divided into sections called segments. They have more complex bodies than other worms. Their blood travels through blood vessels. They have a three-layer body and bilateral symmetry. They have a digestive system with two openings. Food enters through the mouth. Wastes leave through an opening at the other end of the body.

The best-known segmented worm is the earthworm. An earthworm has a head end and a tail end. Every segment of its body, except for the first and last, has four pairs of tiny bristles. These bristles help the earthworm move through the soil.

An earthworm also has complex organ systems that keep it alive. One system breaks down food into nutrients the earthworm can use. Blood is pumped through blood vessels by five pairs of simple hearts. Nerves give the worm information about its surroundings.

THE EARTHWORM

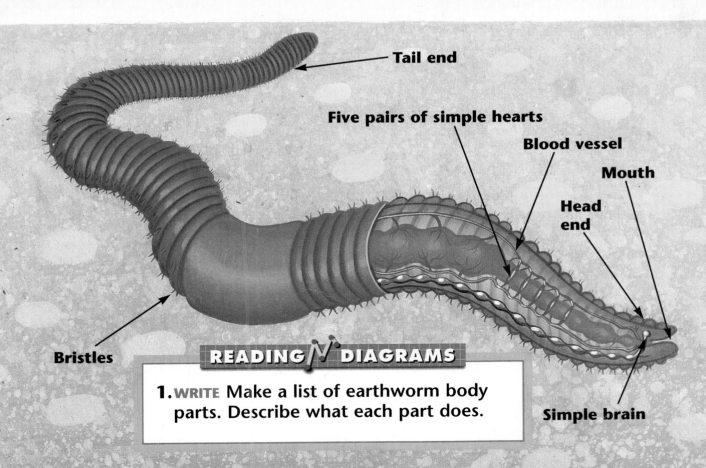

Tail end

Five pairs of simple hearts

Blood vessel

Mouth

Head end

Bristles

Simple brain

READING IN DIAGRAMS

1. WRITE Make a list of earthworm body parts. Describe what each part does.

What Are Some More-Complex Invertebrates?

Mollusks

Do you have a seashell collection? Most seashells come from **mollusks** (mol'əsks). Mollusks are soft-bodied invertebrates. Some, like snails and slugs, live on land. Others, like clams, oysters, and squids, live in water. Most mollusks have bilateral symmetry and many organ systems. Mollusks are among the largest, swiftest, and most intelligent sea animals.

Most mollusk classes have either one shell, two shells, or an inner shell. Snail-like mollusks have one shell. Clamlike mollusks have two shells. The group that includes the octopus and the squid has an inner shell.

This squid is a mollusk that lives in water. There are more than 70,000 different types of mollusks.

Echinoderms

Have you ever seen a sea star? It is an **echinoderm** (i kī'nə dûrm'). Echinoderms are spiny-skinned animals. You can identify most echinoderms by their star design and spiny skin. Echinoderms include sea stars, sand dollars, sea cucumbers, and sea urchins.

Echinoderms have an internal supporting structure called an **endoskeleton** (en'dō skel'i tən). Usually the endoskeleton has many protective spines. A sea star has hard, rounded spines. A sea urchin has long, sharp spines. A sea cucumber does not have spines at all.

Many echinoderms move and grab things with tiny tube feet. Each tube foot is powered by suction.

The sea star uses its arms and tube feet to pry open the oyster. Then it turns its own stomach inside out. It sticks its stomach out to digest the oyster.

What Is the Largest Phylum of Invertebrates?

The largest invertebrate phylum is **arthropods** (är'thrə podz'). It is also the largest of all animal phyla. Arthropods live almost everywhere on Earth. Scientists think there are more than a million arthropod species!

Arthropods have jointed legs and a body that is divided into sections. Some arthropods breathe with gills. Others have an open-tube breathing system.

Arthropods have a hard skeleton on the outside of their bodies called an **exoskeleton** (ek'sō skel'i tən). It protects them and keeps them from drying out. Exoskeletons are made of a light but tough material called *chitin* (kī'tin). An exoskeleton does not grow, but is shed by a process called molting (mōl'ting).

There are more arthropods than all other types of animals combined! You will learn about four main arthropod classes— arachnids (ə rak'nidz), centipedes and millipedes, crustaceans (krus tā'shənz), and insects.

Brain Power

Design your own invertebrate. Give your animal at least one characteristic from each phylum. Draw it, and list its characteristics.

Arachnids

Includes: Spiders, mites, scorpions, ticks, daddy-longlegs
Head: No antennae
Legs and Body: Four pairs of legs, two-section body, up to eight eyes
Home: A wide variety of habitats
Food: Most arachnids are hunters, mainly eating insects.
Special Features: Many arachnids are poisonous, including spiders and scorpions. Some arachnids, such as spiders, can spin webs to trap their food.
Fact: Not all spiders are dangerous. Many are helpful to people. They eat insects and other pests.

Scorpions feed on spiders and insects. Their sting can be dangerous to people.

Crustaceans

Includes: Crabs, lobsters, shrimp, barnacles, crayfish, sow bugs

Head: Jawlike structures for crushing food and chewing; two pairs of antennae for sensing

Legs and Body: Ten or fewer legs, including claws. The body has sections.

Home: Some have ocean and freshwater homes. A few live on land.

Food: Dead animal remains, seaweed, other leftovers

Special Features: Crabs and lobsters can have huge claws. One claw is often much bigger than the other. They use their claws to fight and to scare off predators.

Fact: Millions of shrimp, crabs, and lobsters are eaten every year. Billions of tiny copepods (kō'pə podz) live in the sea. They are the main food for whales and other animals.

Centipedes and Millipedes

Includes: Centipedes, millipedes

Legs and Body: Centipedes: usually less than 100 legs. Millipedes: more than a hundred legs. Both have long, thin, segmented bodies.

Home: Under rocks, in rotting wood and dark, damp places

Food: Centipedes eat worms, slugs, and insects. Millipedes are plant eaters.

How to Tell Them Apart: Centipedes have one pair of legs per segment and can move quickly. Millipedes have two pairs of legs per segment and move slowly.

Facts: Although *centi-* means "100" in Latin, most centipedes have only 30 legs. Some centipedes have poison claws. A millipede's legs move in a wavelike motion.

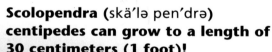

Scolopendra (skä'lə pen'drə) centipedes can grow to a length of 30 centimeters (1 foot)!

Lobsters can live 50 years and grow to lengths of 60 centimeters (2 feet) or more.

Insects

Includes: Beetles, flies, bees, ants, mosquitoes, butterflies, dragonflies, fleas, termites, many others

Head: One pair of antennae

Legs and Body: Three pairs of legs; one or two pairs of wings; three body sections: head, thorax, abdomen

Home: All land habitats, air and freshwater habitats

Food: Other animals and plants

Special Features: A special tube system for breathing; compound eyes made of hundreds of lenses.

Facts: There are more different kinds of insects than there are all other kinds of animals. The first insects appeared about 350 million years ago. Flight speed can reach 58 kilometers (36 miles) per hour. At that speed how far could an insect fly in three hours?

MATH
LINK

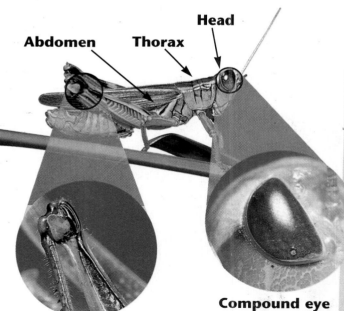

Abdomen   Thorax   Head

Jointed leg

Compound eye

Classifying Invertebrates

HYPOTHESIZE What characteristics would you use to classify these invertebrates? Write a hypothesis in your *Science Journal.*

MATERIALS
• *Science Journal*

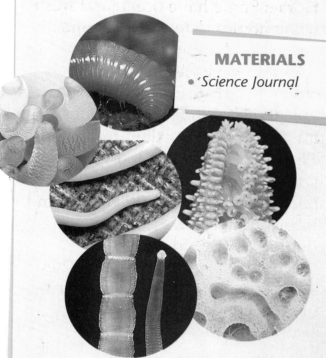

PROCEDURES

1. **IDENTIFY** Use the clues in each picture to identify which type of invertebrate is shown.

2. **COMMUNICATE** Make a table in your *Science Journal* to show how you classified each picture. List key characteristics for each phylum.

CONCLUDE AND APPLY

EXPLAIN How do you know the phylum that each animal belongs to?

What Invertebrates Live in Coral Reefs?

Imagine an animal that forms its own island! Corals do. Coral is made by colonies of polyps. Each polyp looks like a tiny sea anemone. For protection polyps build cup-shaped skeletons around their bodies. When polyps die the skeletons remain. After many years they pile up. A coral reef or island forms.

Coral reefs contain invertebrates of almost every size and shape. A typical reef will have anemones, prawns, worms, lobsters, sea stars, jellyfish, and giant clams. Reefs also have more that 2,000 different kinds of fish—many with brilliant colors and unusual shapes. Coral reefs are among the richest communities on Earth.

Coral reefs are delicate. Coral needs warm, clean water to grow. Unfortunately many coral reefs are threatened by pollution, souvenir hunters, ships, and boats. People take chunks of a coral reef as souvenirs. Ships crash into reefs. Small boats damage reefs with heavy anchors. It may take hundreds of years for the damaged reef to grow back.

What can we do to help protect coral reefs? We can stop pollution, boat carefully, not buy coral souvenirs, and learn more about reefs.

The Great Barrier Reef, located near Australia, is about 2,000 kilometers (1,240 miles) long.

Did you know that most animals on Earth are invertebrates? Between 90 and 95 of every 100 animal species are invertebrates! Invertebrates are important because they are a food source for other animals. People also depend on them for many things. In some parts of the world, mollusks like squids, clams, and oysters are important foods. Earthworms help enrich soil. This helps healthy plants grow. Coral reefs protect islands and provide homes to animals. Water-absorbing sponges have many household uses.

Arthropods also help people. Most people are not allergic to the chitin in an arthropod's exoskeleton. That is why chitin is often used to make contact lenses, artificial skin, and thread for stitches!

Chitin from arthropod exoskeletons has many interesting uses.

REVIEW

1. What is an invertebrate? How can you identify invertebrates?

2. How are segmented worms different from other types of worms?

3. How are echinoderms similar to and different from arthropods?

4. **COMMUNICATE** What kinds of things threaten coral reefs? How can reefs be saved?

5. **CRITICAL THINKING** *Analyze* Which invertebrate phyla have the simplest body systems? Which have the most complex systems?

WHY IT MATTERS **THINK ABOUT IT** What do you think might happen if all the earthworms in an area suddenly died?

WHY IT MATTERS **WRITE ABOUT IT** What if all invertebrates suddenly disappeared? How do you think this would affect life on Earth?

CONTROL

WITHOUT CHEMICALS

What's another name for an insect or a bug? A pest! Farmers know what pests can do to their crops. Some pests stop plant growth. Others cause spots, cracks, lumps, or other marks on fruits and vegetables. How can anyone get rid of these pests? One way is to spray crops with chemical pesticides.

Unfortunately, pesticides themselves are a problem. They can kill fish, bees and other helpful insects, and can make humans sick, too. That's why it's important to carefully wash any pesticides off fruits and vegetables before you eat them.

Can you safely control pests? Sure, paper or plastic around fruit trees will stop some insects. Electric light traps can destroy other pests. Scientists use radiation on male insects. When the males mate, any eggs the females lay won't hatch! That cuts down on the pest population.

Science, Technology, and Society

Insects can also be used to kill other insects. Some wasps eat the larva of problem insects. Some bacteria and other organisms also feed on problem insects.

Scientists continue to look for ways to eliminate pests and help useful insects survive. It's important to control insects, but scientists know it's more important to keep a balance in nature.

Better insect control could help to cut America's use of pesticides down. Then we could grow pest-free food and also keep harmful chemicals out of our food, our water, and our air.

DISCUSSION STARTER

1. How can insects be controlled without using pesticides?

2. Pesticides can be dangerous. Why do people still use them?

To learn more about harmful pesticides, visit *www.mhschool.com/science* and enter the keyword PESTS.

*inter*NET
CONNECTION

SCIENCE WORDS

cold-blooded describes an animal with a body temperature that changes with its surroundings

warm-blooded describes an animal with a constant body temperature

amphibian a cold-blooded vertebrate that spends part of its life in water and part of its life on land

reptile a cold-blooded vertebrate that lives on land and has waterproof skin with scales or plates

mammal a warm-blooded vertebrate with hair or fur that feeds milk to its young

Animals with Backbones

Did you know that you are classified into the same large group as fish, toads, snakes, birds, and rabbits? What could you all possibly have in common?

All these animals have a backbone. They are classified into a large group known as vertebrates. However, these animals are also very different from one another. These differences are used to make smaller groups.

EXPLORE

HYPOTHESIZE **What characteristics are used to classify vertebrates? Write a hypothesis in your *Science Journal*. How could you test your ideas?**

Investigate What Vertebrates Are Like

Observe some vertebrates. What characteristics set each of these animals apart from the others?

PROCEDURES

▨ **Safety:** Be careful with live animals.

OBSERVE As you observe each animal, look for answers to these questions. Record your observations in your *Science Journal*. If you like, you can record sounds or take photographs to better observe these animals.

a. Where does it live—in water, on land, or both?

b. What color is it?

c. What kind of outer covering does it have?

d. What body parts does it have?

e. Do you see eyes, ears, nostrils, or other sense organs?

f. How does it move?

CONCLUDE AND APPLY

1. COMMUNICATE What major characteristics did you observe in each animal?

2. COMPARE What are the main differences between a fish and a frog?

3. COMPARE What are the major differences between a bird and a hamster?

GOING FURTHER: Problem Solving

4. IDENTIFY Which animal are you most like in this activity? Why do you think so?

MATERIALS

- goldfish
- frog
- chameleon, turtle, or lizard
- parakeet
- hamster, gerbil, or guinea pig
- hand lens
- camera (optional)
- tape recorder (optional)
- *Science Journal*

235

What Are Vertebrates Like?

The Explore Activity showed several vertebrates. Although they have very different characteristics, they all have a backbone that is part of the endoskeleton made of bones.

An endoskeleton has two important jobs. First, it supports the body. It also protects the soft inner organs.

Classifying Vertebrates

The animal kingdom is divided into the invertebrate phylum and the chordate phylum. Vertebrates are part of the chordate phylum. Most chordates are vertebrates.

Vertebrates are divided into seven classes based on characteristics such as body structure.

Vertebrates are also classified by how they control body temperature.

Fish, amphibians, and reptiles are **cold-blooded** (kōld′blud′id). A cold-blooded animal gets heat from outside its body. Its body temperature changes with the temperature of its surroundings.

Birds and mammals are **warm-blooded** (wôrm′blud′id). Their body temperature doesn't change much. They use the energy from food to keep a constant body temperature.

Brain Power

How is an endoskeleton different from an exoskeleton?

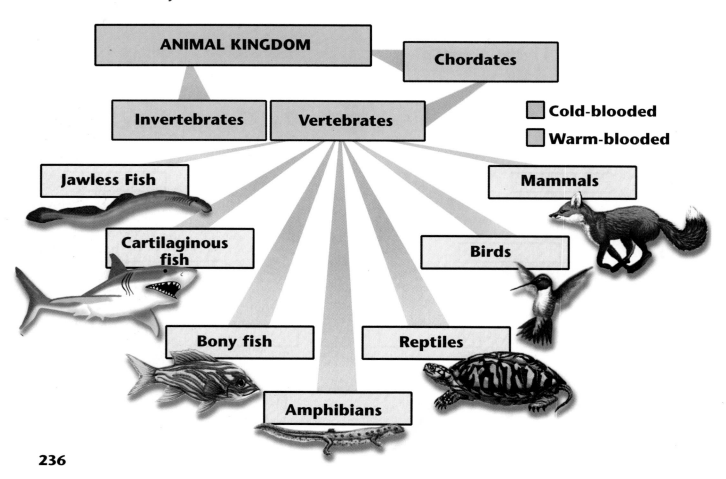

ANIMAL KINGDOM

Chordates

Invertebrates   Vertebrates

☐ Cold-blooded
☐ Warm-blooded

Jawless Fish

Cartilaginous fish

Bony fish

Amphibians

Mammals

Birds

Reptiles

What Are the Characteristics of Fish?

There are three classes of fish—jawless fish, *cartilaginous* (kär′tə laj′ə nəs) *fish*, and bony fish. All fish have several characteristics.

- Fish are cold-blooded vertebrates that live in fresh or salt water.
- Fish have streamlined bodies and gills for breathing.
- Gills take oxygen out of water the way your lungs take oxygen out of the air. They also get rid of carbon dioxide.

GENERAL FISH CHARACTERISTICS

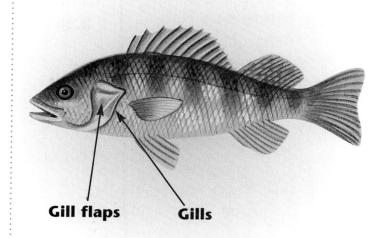

Gill flaps   **Gills**

Jawless Fish

What is the first thing you notice about these fish? They do not look anything like other fish! These eel-like animals are jawless fish.

Jawless fish are soft, slimy, and vicious. Instead of jaws they have powerful suckerlike mouths. A jawless fish uses its mouth to attach itself to its prey. It uses a horn tooth to cut a hole in its prey. Then it slowly sucks out the fluids and insides of the prey.

Jawless fish include lampreys and hagfish. These fish have no scales and unusual fins. Their bodies have a rubbery cartilage skeleton. Cartilage is a tough, flexible tissue. Your outer ears are made of cartilage.

Most lampreys, like these, live in fresh water.

What Are the Other Classes of Fish?

Cartilaginous Fish

The major characteristic of a cartilaginous fish is a skeleton made entirely of cartilage. Cartilaginous fish also have movable jaws, fins, and tough, sandpaper-like skin.

Rays, skates and sharks are cartilaginous fish. Sharks are keen hunters. They can smell blood in the water from many meters away. With their razor-sharp teeth, sharks can tear apart their prey in seconds. Most sharks, however, do not attack people. They feed on small fish and invertebrates.

Bony Fish

Have you ever gone fishing? If you ever caught a fish, it most likely was a fish from this class. Bony fish are the largest vertebrate class. They have jaws and skeletons made of bone. More than 21,000 different kinds of bony fish swim both in the ocean and in fresh water.

What makes bony fish so successful? Tough, overlapping scales protect their skin. Gill flaps protect their gills. Fins help the fish steer in the water.

Bony fish have different body plans. Predator fish have sleek bodies and powerful muscles. Reef fish have box-shaped bodies that fit in small spaces. Bottom dwellers are flat. Eels have snakelike shapes to fit into tight spaces.

Rays are bottom dwellers that eat invertebrates. This manta ray can grow to a length of more than 6 meters (20 feet).

The cichlid (sik'lid) fish keeps its eggs in its mouth until the fish hatch. What type of advantage does this give the young fish?

What Are Amphibians?

Have you ever seen a frog, toad, or salamander? If you have, how would you describe it? Frogs, toads, and salamanders are amphibians (am fib′ē ənz). An amphibian is a cold-blooded vertebrate that spends part of its life in water and part of its life on land.

Amphibians start out their lives in the water. A tadpole is a young frog. It has gills and fins. It cannot live on land because it has no lungs or legs. Over time the tadpole turns into a frog. It loses its gills and breathes through lungs and its skin. It also loses its fins and grows legs.

Although adult frogs live most of their lives on land, they are never far from water. An amphibian's skin will dry out without water. That is why amphibians live in wet or damp places.

Do you know how to tell a frog from a toad? This table will help you.

This is a young tadpole.

Frog or Toad?		
	Frog	**Toad**
Body	sleek	plump
Movement	jump	hop
Skin	moist and smooth	dry and bumpy

With time a tadpole changes and grows into a frog.

READING TABLES

WRITE Write a short paragraph comparing and contrasting the characteristics of a frog and a toad.

What Are the Characteristics of Reptiles?

Do you think that a snake has slimy skin? Some people think that **reptiles** (rep′ təlz) like snakes are slimy. In fact reptile skin is dry. Reptiles have skin with scales or larger plates. Strong, waterproof skin helped reptiles become the first vertebrate group to live on land.

Reptiles are cold-blooded animals with a backbone and an endoskeleton. How could they survive on land when other vertebrates could not? Reptiles have lungs. Their skin keeps water from escaping out of their bodies. Their eggs are tougher than amphibian eggs. All of these traits helped reptiles become successful on land.

Reptiles can be classified into four smaller groups, called orders. There are four main reptile orders—tuataras (tü′ə tär′əz), turtles, lizards and snakes, and alligators and crocodiles.

Tuataras are the smallest order. There are only two members, both of which are endangered. Tuataras live on islands off New Zealand.

Turtles and tortoises are among the longest-living animals. Some tortoises live more than 100 years. Sea turtles can swim at speeds of 9 kilometers (6 miles) per hour.

Lizards and snakes outnumber the other groups. Most lizards have limbs, although a few types do not. Lizards are insect eaters. Snakes are meat eaters. Some snakes kill their prey by squeezing them, others use poison. More than 500 species of snakes are poisonous.

Dinosaurs were reptiles that walked on Earth for 150 million years. They disappeared about 66 million years ago. Today crocodiles and alligators are their closest living relatives. A large adult crocodile can weigh as much as 900 kilograms (1 ton) and eat prey as large as deer. Without a backbone, these large animals would not be able to support their weight on land.

Tuataras are not very different from their prehistoric ancestors.

What Are the Characteristics of Birds?

Birds are vertebrates with several distinct characteristics.

- Birds have feathers. Feathers are light but very warm. Some birds have feathers with dull colors. This allows them to blend into their surroundings and hide from enemies. Others have bright colors to attract mates.

- Birds have beaks without teeth. Some birds, like finches, have a beak designed for eating seeds. A meat-eating bird like a hawk has a sharp, curved beak for tearing flesh. A flamingo has a beak designed for catching fish.

- Birds have two legs with clawed feet. Birds have scales on their feet, like reptiles. A bird's feet are well designed for its needs. Hawks have sharp claws for catching and tearing prey. A penguin has flat feet for walking. Birds like swifts have tiny feet. They spend most of their time flying, not perching.

- Birds are warm-blooded like you.

- Birds lay eggs with strong shells. Most birds sit on their eggs to keep them warm until they hatch.

- All birds have wings. However, not all birds can fly. Penguins and ostriches cannot fly, but this is not a problem. Ostriches can run at speeds up to 72 kilometers (45 miles) per hour! Penguins are excellent swimmers.

The wings of a frigate bird measure more than 200 centimeters (80 inches) across, yet its entire skeleton weighs only a little more than 100 grams (4 ounces)! Frigate birds can fly at speeds of more than 150 kilometers (95 miles) per hour.

- Most birds can fly. A bird's body is designed for flight. Bird bones are hollow and thin. Bird lungs and flight muscles are powerful. Bird feathers are strong and light. They fit together to form an air-tight wing surface. Together these features help birds fly.

There are four main bird groups. One group includes perching birds, like the robin. The second group includes water birds, like the duck. The third group includes predator, or hunting, birds, like the hawk. The fourth group includes flight-less birds, like the penguin.

What Are the Characteristics of Mammals?

How would you describe the characteristics of a human? Make a list. The characteristics you named describe a **mammal** (mam′ əl). You and about 4,000 different vertebrates are classified as mammals.

What is a mammal? A mammal is a warm-blooded vertebrate with three major characteristics. How do the characteristics you named compare with this list?

1. Most mammals have body hair or fur.
2. Females feed milk to their young.
3. All but a few mammals are born live rather than hatching from an egg.

On land the fastest animal is a mammal, the cheetah. The tallest land animal is a mammal, the giraffe. The largest and heaviest creature in the animal kingdom is also a mammal, the blue whale.

Types of Mammals

There are three basic types of mammals. Mammals that lay eggs make up one group. Members of this group include the platypus and spiny anteater. After the young hatch, they drink milk made by the female's body.

The second group includes animals with pouches. Members of this group include koalas, kangaroos,

Mammals like this platypus and her young live in distant parts of Tasmania, Australia, and New Guinea.

and opossums. The female has a pouch that holds the immature offspring until it is fully developed.

The third group includes animals like cats, horses, whales, bats, mice, apes, and you. All of these animals have offspring that develop inside the female's body. Most mammals are born at a well-developed stage. Larger mammals generally develop inside the female's body longer than smaller mammals. For example, rabbits have offspring after 30 days. A rhinoceros takes over a year to develop before it is born.

Where Do Mammals Live?

Mammals live in almost every kind of habitat and move in almost every kind of way. The horse lives on land and walks on legs. The walrus lives in salt water and swims. Bats live in caves and fly through the air. Gophers are mammals that live underground. Otters are mammals that live in fresh water and swim.

An interesting mammal from the past lived on what is now Seymour Island, near the Antarctic Peninsula. This mammal was a giant relative of the armadillo. It had an armored tail and was about the size and shape of a small car! The plates that covered its body were different sizes. Some were as small as a saucer, others were as big as a dinner plate. Scientists think that this animal lived near streams and ate plants. Mammals really are an interesting class of vertebrates!

This ancient mammal was nearly as big as a small car!

Classifying Vertebrates

HYPOTHESIZE What characteristics would you use to classify these vertebrates? Write a hypothesis in your *Science Journal*.

MATERIALS
• *Science Journal*

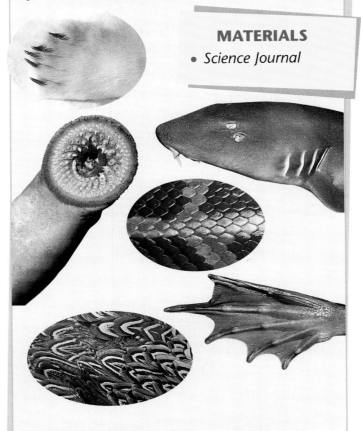

PROCEDURES

1. **CLASSIFY** Use the clues in each picture to help you classify each animal.

2. **COMMUNICATE** Make a table in your *Science Journal* to show how you classified each picture.

CONCLUDE AND APPLY

EXPLAIN How do you know which class each animal belongs to?

243

How Can Animals Help People?

People are warm-blooded mammals who sometimes get ill or become sad. When people have troubles, animals can often help.

Duffy is a dog who is part of a program called Pet Partners. Every week Duffy and other Pet Partners go to hospitals and other places. Their job is to help people who are very sick, sad, or lonely feel better.

How did Duffy get to become a Pet Partner? It wasn't easy. First, Duffy needed to pass many different tests. Testers put food in front of Duffy. They bounced balls in front of him. They even brought in other dogs to distract him. In each case Duffy had to stay still until his trainer told him it was okay to move.

After Duffy passed all his tests, he needed to be trained. During his training Duffy learned how to help people. He learned to be patient with strangers. He learned how to be gentle with young children and very old people. After four months of training, Duffy was ready to be a Pet Partner.

Pet Partners work in hospitals and nursing homes. Do Pet Partners really help people? Take a look at the smile you see on this page!

Duffy wears a special uniform. He has a blue harness and a special badge that says, "I am a visiting dog."

Compare the size of this blue whale's backbone to the man in the picture.

WHY IT MATTERS

How does a backbone make a difference? Think about the invertebrates and vertebrates you have studied. Invertebrates are generally small. Many vertebrates are very large, like the rhinoceros, the great white shark, and the polar bear. This is no coincidence. Backbones and endoskeletons give animals support. This support allows vertebrates to grow to very large sizes. That is why the largest animals on Earth are vertebrates.

The blue whale can weigh up to 150 metric tons (165 tons). How many pounds is that?

MATH LINK

REVIEW

1. How are vertebrates different from invertebrates?

2. What is the difference between the three types of fish?

3. How can a Pet Partner help people?

4. EXPLAIN Why is a platypus classified as a mammal even though it lays eggs?

5. CRITICAL THINKING *Analyze* A newt looks like a lizard, but it is an amphibian. What traits must a newt have?

WHY IT MATTERS THINK ABOUT IT
Droopy Dogs are made only out of clay. They have a problem—they droop. Big Droopy Dogs can't hold up their own weight. How could you fix them?

WHY IT MATTERS WRITE ABOUT IT
Write a short paragraph about how you would fix Droopy Dogs. Try it. Does it work?

READING SKILL Make an outline showing how animals are classified as invertebrates or vertebrates. Include an example of each and its characteristics.

HELPING ENDANGERED ANIMALS

What's that gliding through the water? It's a manatee. This mammal spends its days slowly munching grasses in the water. That's why manatees are also called "sea cows!"

Unfortunately, people hunted the manatee. Its tough hide was used for making shoes and canoes. Oil from its body was burned in lamps. Its bones had many uses, and the animal could be eaten.

In Florida, where most manatees live, it's illegal to hunt them. Still, manatees are endangered. Trash poisons their water. Fishing nets trap them. Boat propellers scar or kill them.

Many manatees are identified by their scars. Some are equipped with radio transmitters so researchers can track them. When researchers find sick or injured manatees, they nurse them back to health.

Making a Difference

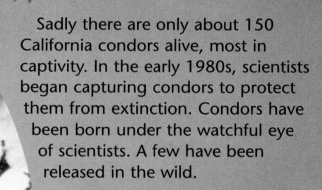

The California condor is the largest flying land bird in North America. It has a wingspan of about 2.5–3.1 meters (8–10 feet). Once thousands of these graceful giants soared over the wilds of southern California. Now much of that territory has been developed. Hunting and poisoning by pesticides also pushed the condor close to extinction.

Sadly there are only about 150 California condors alive, most in captivity. In the early 1980s, scientists began capturing condors to protect them from extinction. Condors have been born under the watchful eye of scientists. A few have been released in the wild.

DISCUSSION STARTER

1. What is killing manatees today?

2. Why would it be important to track manatees and condors?

To learn more about manatees and condors, visit *www.mhschool.com/science* and enter the keyword INDANGER.

*inter*NET
CONNECTION

SCIENCE WORDS

arthropod p. 227

cnidarian p. 223

cold-
   blooded p. 236

echinoderm p. 226

endo-
   skeleton p. 226

exoskeleton p. 227

food web p. 213

invertebrate p. 214

mollusk p. 226

symmetry p. 214

vertebrate p. 214

warm-
   blooded p. 236

USING SCIENCE WORDS

Number a paper from 1 to 10. Fill in 1 to 5 with words from the list above.

1. An animal that has a constant body temperature is called ___?___.

2. One example of a soft-bodied invertebrate is a(n) ___?___.

3. An animal with a backbone is called a(n) ___?___.

4. An inner supporting structure is called a(n) ___?___.

5. The hard covering that protects an invertebrate's body is a(n) ___?___.

6–10. Pick five words from the list above that were not used in 1 to 5, and use each in a sentence.

UNDERSTANDING SCIENCE IDEAS

11. What is the difference between a mammal and a reptile?

12. What are the major characteristics of birds?

USING IDEAS AND SKILLS

13. **OBSERVE** Make a chart that shows the symmetry of ten different animals.

14. **READING SKILL: OUTLINING** Scientists group living things according to similar characteristics. Explain how this helps them study all the animals in the world. Make an outline of the groups and characteristics scientists use.

15. **THINKING LIKE A SCIENTIST** All very large invertebrates, like the giant squid, live underwater. Can you explain why they don't live on land?

MATH
LINK

PROBLEMS and PUZZLES

Thumbprint Symmetry Use an inkpad and white paper to make a thumbprint. Does it have symmetry? Use the reflection of a mirror to find out. Stand a mirror with a straight edge in the middle of the print. Try this method to see if other natural objects have symmetry.

Stand a mirror here.

CHAPTER 8
SEE HOW THEY
WORK

How do you think this animal gets food? What parts of its body does the animal use to get food? Besides getting food, what else does this animal do to survive? How do the organs in its body work together keeping this animal alive? In this chapter, you'll find out how organs work together.

In this chapter you will locate details that support a main idea. As an example you may use details to describe how a fish can get oxygen underwater.

WHY IT MATTERS

Organ systems work together to keep animals alive.

SCIENCE WORDS

circulatory system the organ system that moves blood through the body

respiratory system the organ system that brings oxygen to body cells and removes waste gas

excretory system the organ system that removes liquid wastes

digestive system the organ system that breaks down food for fuel

skeletal system the organ system made up of bones

muscular system the organ system made up of muscles that move bones

nervous system the organ system that controls all other body systems

Organ Systems

How are a fish and a frog similar and different? Think about their bodies and where they live. The frog is a more complex animal than a fish. A frog breathes with lungs instead of gills. A frog has limbs instead of fins. A frog can live both on land and in water. Do you think a frog also has more complex organs and organ systems than a fish?

EXPLORE

HYPOTHESIZE Which do you think is more complex—a frog's heart or a fish's heart? Write a hypothesis in your *Science Journal.* How could you test your ideas?

Investigate How Blood Travels

Compare models of fish and amphibian hearts.

MATERIALS

- 5 straws
- two 7-oz cups, each with a hole in the bottom
- three $3\frac{1}{2}$-oz cups, each with a hole in the bottom
- 2 paper circles
- 5 labels
- marking pen
- tape
- *Science Journal*

PROCEDURES

1. Label each small cup "atrium." Label each large cup "ventricle."

2. **MAKE A MODEL: FISH HEART** Tape the paper circle with one flap over the top of one ventricle. Center the top of an atrium over the flap in the circle. Tape it to the paper.

3. Label one straw "From gills and body." Place it in the hole in the bottom of the atrium. Label another straw "To gills and body." Place it in the hole in the bottom of the ventricle. Draw the model in your *Science Journal*.

4. **MAKE A MODEL: AMPHIBIAN HEART** Tape the paper circle with two flaps over the top of a ventricle. Center the top of an atrium over each flap. Tape the cups to the paper.

5. Label one straw "From the body." Place it in the hole in the bottom of the right cup. Label another straw "From lungs." Place it in the hole in the bottom of the left cup. Label the third straw "To lungs and body." Place it in the hole in the paper between the two small cups. Draw the model.

This is a model of a fish heart.

This is a model of an amphibian heart.

CONCLUDE AND APPLY

COMPARE AND CONTRAST How are the fish heart and the amphibian heart alike? Different?

How Does Blood Travel?

Do you know what blood is? Blood is a liquid tissue made up mostly of red blood cells, white blood cells, and a liquid called *plasma* (plaz′mə). Blood carries food, oxygen, and water to the body's cells and removes wastes from cells.

The heart is part of an organ system called the **circulatory system** (sûr′kyə lə tôr′ē sis′təm). The circulatory system's job is to move blood through the body.

Sponges and cnidarians don't need a circulatory system because materials can move freely in and out of each thin body layer. Insects and other invertebrates have open circulatory systems. The heart simply bathes the tissues in blood, which slowly drains back to the heart.

All vertebrates have a closed circulatory system, where blood travels through tubes called blood vessels. Some of the more complex invertebrates, like the earthworm, also have a closed system.

As the Explore Activity showed, complex animals have complex hearts. A fish has a simple heart with two parts, or chambers. It allows blood carrying wastes and oxygen to mix. An amphibian has a heart with three chambers. The most complex animals, mammals, have hearts with four chambers. They do not allow blood carrying waste gas to mix with blood carrying oxygen.

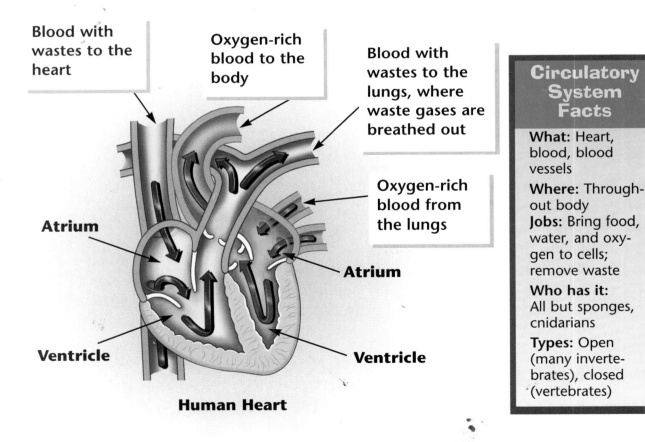

Blood with wastes to the heart

Oxygen-rich blood to the body

Blood with wastes to the lungs, where waste gases are breathed out

Oxygen-rich blood from the lungs

Atrium

Atrium

Ventricle

Ventricle

Human Heart

Circulatory System Facts

What: Heart, blood, blood vessels

Where: Throughout body

Jobs: Bring food, water, and oxygen to cells; remove waste

Who has it: All but sponges, cnidarians

Types: Open (many invertebrates), closed (vertebrates)

How Do Animals Get Oxygen?

Cells need the oxygen carried by blood to get energy from food. The **respiratory system** (res′pər ə tôr′ē sis′təm) brings oxygen to body cells and removes the waste gas carbon dioxide. Respiratory systems become more complex in more complex animals.

Most invertebrates don't have a specialized respiratory system at all. Their bodies usually are small, and gases can easily move in and out of tissues, even through their skin. An insect's exoskeleton has holes connected to tubes that bring oxygen to different tissues.

Larger, more complex animals and animals with waterproof skin need a respiratory system. Each has a respiratory system well designed for its body and where it lives. Fish and young amphibians, such as tadpoles, have gills that take oxygen out of the water and get rid of carbon dioxide. Adult amphibians breathe through both their skin and lungs.

How You Breathe

What do you think causes you to breathe in and out between 12 and 16 times per minute? The plastic bottle on the right is a good model.

Mammals have a muscle called the *diaphragm* (dī′ə fram′) below the lungs. When relaxed the diaphragm pushes up. Air leaves the lungs. When the diaphragm flattens and pulls down, the lungs fill with air.

Respiratory System Facts
What: Lungs, gills, skin
Where: Open to outer air
Jobs: Bring oxygen into body, remove waste gases out of body
Who has it: Vertebrates, large invertebrates, insects
Works with: The circulatory system to move gases in and out

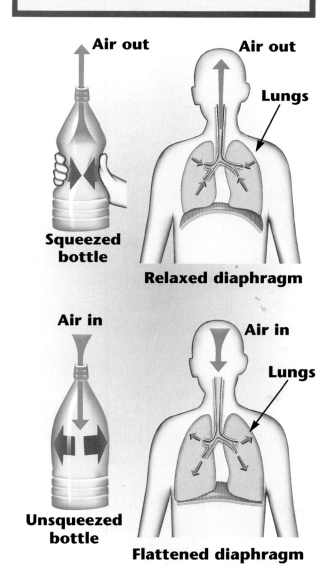

Air out — Air out — Lungs — Squeezed bottle — Relaxed diaphragm

Air in — Air in — Lungs — Unsqueezed bottle — Flattened diaphragm

Brain Power

Why does air leave the lungs when the diaphragm relaxes?

How Do Liquid Wastes Leave the Body?

Animals create many types of wastes. The waste gas carbon dioxide is removed from the body by the lungs. Liquid wastes, created when cells break down chemicals, are removed by the **excretory system** (ek′skri tôr′ē sis′təm).

Animals get rid of liquid wastes in different ways. In thin-layered animals such as sponges, wastes simply wash away. Flatworms and earthworms have tubules into which wastes drain and are passed from the body.

More complex animals have excretory systems well designed for their bodies and where they live. For example, most reptiles live in dry places. To keep from losing water, their kidneys turn wastes into a dry paste. Amphibians live in or near water at all times. Their *urine* (yur′in) is more wet than the wastes of reptiles. Birds do not store wastes in a bladder. They turn their wastes into a paste that is eliminated from the body with solid wastes.

In vertebrates the main waste-removal organs are the two *kidneys* (kid′nēz). Each kidney filters wastes from the blood. These wastes are concentrated into a liquid called urine. Urine is stored in the *bladder* (blad′ər) until it is removed from the body.

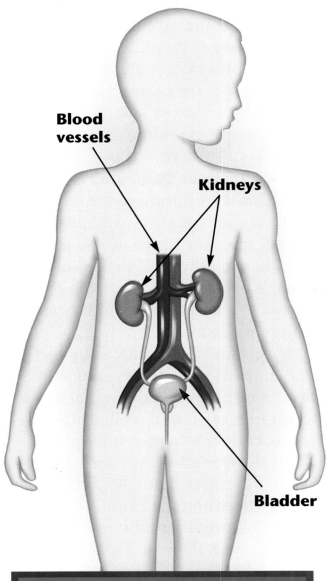

Blood from the body enters the kidneys. The kidneys filter out wastes.

Blood vessels

Kidneys

Bladder

Excretory System Facts

What: Kidneys, special cells, tubules

Where: Different body locations

Jobs: Remove liquid wastes from the body

Who has it: Vertebrates, some invertebrates

Works with: The circulatory system to filter blood

How Is Food Broken Down?

Before body cells can use food for energy, it must be broken down. That is the job of the **digestive system** (di jes'tiv sis'təm).

In simple animals like sponges and cnidarians, cells along the body walls break down food into small particles. These cells transfer the particles to cells in the body.

Other simple invertebrates, like some flatworms, have a digestive system with one opening. Food enters through the mouth. Wastes and undigested food leave through the same opening.

A segmented worm has a digestive system with two openings. Food enters through the mouth. Wastes exit through the other end of the body.

Birds do not chew food. A muscular organ called a *gizzard* (giz'ərd) stores pebbles that grind food before it enters the rest of the system.

What happens to your food?

HUMAN DIGESTIVE SYSTEM

1 Food is broken down by teeth and saliva.

2 It passes to the stomach through the *esophagus.*

3 Acids break down the food. Stomach muscles mix it.

Mouth

Esophagus

Liver

Stomach

Large intestine

Small intestine

4 Food passes into the *small intestine.* Chemicals from the liver and other glands mix with the food. When it is digested, nutrients are absorbed into the blood through the small intestine's walls.

5 Solid wastes are passed to the *large intestine.*

Digestive System Facts

What: Teeth, saliva, esophagus, stomach, intestines, liver, glands
Where: Hollow tube through body
Job: Break down food
How: Chewing, grinding, squeezing, chemicals
Types: One or two openings
Who has it: Vertebrates, most invertebrates
Works with: Circulatory system

How Do Animals Move?

A vertebrate's bones form its **skeletal system** (skel'i təl sis'təm). Bones are living tissues. Minerals make bones hard. The skeletal system supports the body and protects body organs. It works with the **muscular system** (mus'kyə lər sis'təm) to allow a vertebrate to move. The muscular system is made of the body's muscles. Muscles are tough tissues that can move.

How do invertebrates move? Almost all invertebrates that can move have some kind of muscle tissue. An earthworm shortens and stretches its body to move.

In vertebrates muscles produce movement by shortening and pulling on bones. Vertebrates use bones and muscles together to move in different ways. Powerful muscles allow a fish to wriggle back and forth as it swims. A snake uses its muscles to slither along. Its bones are designed to wriggle as its muscles shorten and relax.

HUMAN MUSCULAR AND SKELETAL SYSTEMS

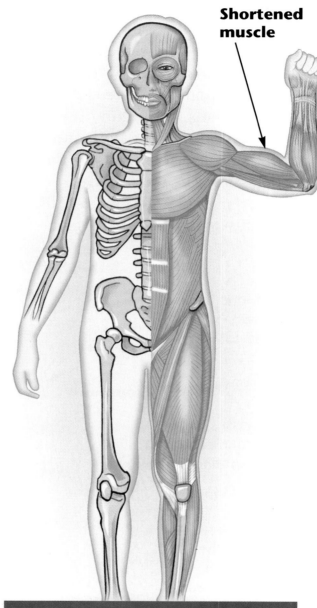

Shortened muscle

Muscular and Skeletal Systems Facts

What: Bones, muscles, cartilage
Where: Entire body
Jobs: Support, protection, movement
Types: Exoskeleton and endoskeleton
Who has it: Vertebrates and some invertebrates
Works with: Nervous system

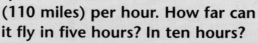

DID YOU KNOW?

Birds have powerful muscles in their chests. Some use them to fly at incredible speeds. A racing pigeon can fly at speeds of 177 kilometers (110 miles) per hour. How far can it fly in five hours? In ten hours?

MATH LINK

How Do Animals Control Organ Systems?

How do animals sense changes in their world and control their organ systems? The **nervous system** (nûr′vəs sis′təm) is the body's master control system. A nervous system is made of nerve cells and nerves. More complex animals have a brain and some or all of the senses—seeing, tasting, hearing, touching, and smelling.

Simple animals have simple nervous systems. More complicated animals have more complicated nervous systems. Vertebrates have the most complex nervous systems.

The structure of an animal's nervous system relates to its lifestyle. Compare the parts of the brain related to the senses of sight and smell in these three organisms.

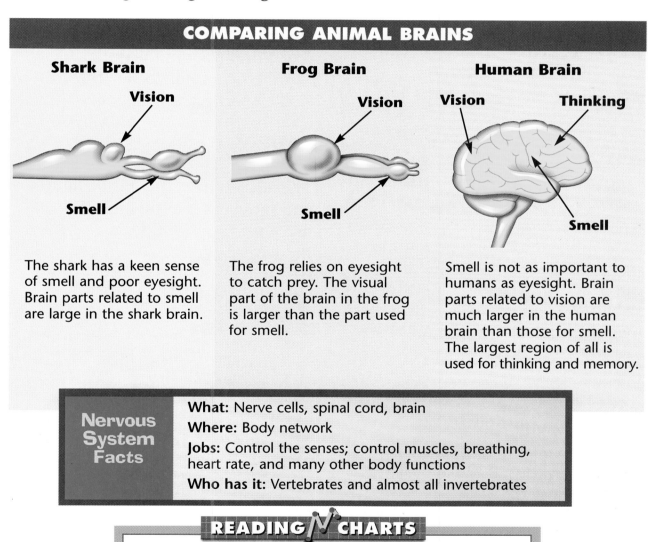

COMPARING ANIMAL BRAINS

Shark Brain
Vision
Smell

The shark has a keen sense of smell and poor eyesight. Brain parts related to smell are large in the shark brain.

Frog Brain
Vision
Smell

The frog relies on eyesight to catch prey. The visual part of the brain in the frog is larger than the part used for smell.

Human Brain
Vision
Thinking
Smell

Smell is not as important to humans as eyesight. Brain parts related to vision are much larger in the human brain than those for smell. The largest region of all is used for thinking and memory.

Nervous System Facts

What: Nerve cells, spinal cord, brain
Where: Body network
Jobs: Control the senses; control muscles, breathing, heart rate, and many other body functions
Who has it: Vertebrates and almost all invertebrates

READING CHARTS

REPRESENT Draw or make your own models to help you compare these brains.

Fooling Your Senses

HYPOTHESIZE Can your eyes be fooled? Write a hypothesis in your *Science Journal*.

A

MATERIALS
• *Science Journal*

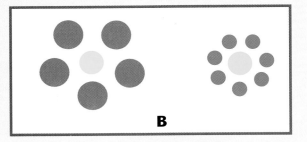

B

PROCEDURES

1. OBSERVE Look at drawing A. What do you see?

2. OBSERVE Observe the center circles in drawing B. Compare their sizes by just observing.

3. MEASURE Measure each yellow circle in drawing B. Which yellow circle is bigger?

CONCLUDE AND APPLY

DRAW CONCLUSIONS Can your eyes fool you? Explain.

Do Some Animals Have Special Sense Organs?

Do you think an animal can "see" with its ears? A bat can. Many animals, like bats, have specialized sense organs that collect information about their surroundings. For example, a bat makes a series of clicking sounds, then listens for echoes. A click makes certain echo patterns when it bounces off different objects. A bat can detect these changes with its ears. Using echoes it can find prey in the dark.

Can an animal "taste" the air? A snake's forked tongue collects tiny odor particles. These particles tell where prey or enemies are.

An insect eye has many lenses. This allows an insect to see light and movement in several directions, but not a clear image. To an insect the world probably looks like a newspaper photo viewed through a hand lens. Try it.

The lenses in an insect eye focus an image on many spots.

What do you think the line of small holes along this fish's body does? Cells along the line have tiny hairs. When the hairs move, the fish knows the water is disturbed. This helps the fish sense tiny waves in the water to detect prey or enemies.

lateral line

Everything you do depends on organ systems. Think what happens when you kick a ball. Your nervous system sees the ball and sends a message to kick. Your circulatory system brings food and oxygen from your digestive and respiratory systems to your foot. Then your skeletal and muscular systems kick the ball! Understanding the parts that make up your organ systems and how they work lets you take good care of them.

Specialized cells along this fish's body give it information about nearby objects.

REVIEW

1. Name and describe the function of seven body systems. Which system controls all of the other systems?

2. What is the difference between an open and a closed circulatory system?

3. How does a bat use its ears to "see"? How is this different from the way you use your ears?

4. **COMPARE** Which body systems get rid of wastes? How are they different?

5. **CRITICAL THINKING** *Analyze* How are body systems different from one animal group to another? Which animals have simple body systems? More complicated body systems?

WHY IT MATTERS THINK ABOUT IT
Suppose you could shrink to microscopic size and take a tour of one of your body systems. Which system would you choose? Why?

WHY IT MATTERS WRITE ABOUT IT
Describe what your tour would be like. Draw pictures to add to your description.

259

HELP WANTED:

Animal Doctor

Love working with animals? A veterinarian may be the career for you. First, you must complete two to four years of college. Then you apply to a veterinary college.

The United States has nearly 30 veterinary schools and colleges. Most veterinary schools offer a four-year program. In order to be a licensed vet, students must pass a state test and one or more national tests.

Most vets work with sick or injured pets. Some vets treat only zoo animals. Others help only farm animals. They might work on a cattle ranch or a large chicken farm.

Would it surprise you to know that some animals treat themselves? Dr. Eloy Rodriguez is a famous biochemist who works and travels all over the world. His specialty is studying the

It appeared that these chimps were eating healing substances. They were practicing "self-medication." Dr. Rodriguez tries to create these natural healing substances in the laboratory. His goal is to make these remedies available for human diseases.

DISCUSSION STARTER

1. Why do so many people want to be vets? Would you like to work with animals?

2. How do you think the chimps knew which plants to eat?

natural chemicals that plants and animals produce. He tries to discover how the chemicals work.

During a trip to the rain forests of Africa, Dr. Rodriguez noticed that sick chimpanzees ate plants that didn't taste good. He analyzed these plants and found that they contained substances that were poisonous to fungi and certain viruses.

To learn more about veterinarians, visit **www.mhschool.com/science** and enter the keyword VETS.

*inter***NET CONNECTION**

WHY IT MATTERS

Animals develop and reproduce in many interesting ways.

SCIENCE WORDS

metamorphosis is a process of changes during certain animals' development

life cycle the stages of an animal's growth and change

life span how long an animal can be expected to live

asexual reproduction produces offspring with only one parent

sexual reproduction produces offspring with two parents

heredity the passing of traits from parent to offspring

Development and Reproduction

What observations can you make of this dog and her puppies?

You may notice that some puppies have colors different from their mother. They are also all smaller than their mother. Even though the puppies are different from their mother in some ways, they all look like a small copy of an adult dog. Do all animals look like small copies of their parents?

EXPLORE

HYPOTHESIZE Do you know of young animals that look very different from their parents? How do you think they change as they grow older? Write a hypothesis in your *Science Journal*. How could you test your ideas?

EXPLORE ACTIVITY

Design Your Own Experiment

HOW DO MEALWORMS CHANGE AS THEY GROW?

PROCEDURES

1. **OBSERVE** As a group choose a Mealworm Observation Station that your teacher has set up. Each station has three jars labeled A–C.

2. **OBSERVE** Break into smaller groups. Each group should observe the animals in one jar. Record your observations in your *Science Journal*. Share your observations with the other members of your larger group.

3. **ASK QUESTIONS** Record any questions you have about mealworms and how they change and grow. How could you find the answers?

4. **EXPERIMENT** Design simple experiments to find out as much as you can about the mealworms. Do they prefer light or dark places? Damp or dry places? Make a group table to display your findings.

5. **OBSERVE** Make observations of the animals every few days. Record your observations. Draw the different stages of development that you observe.

CONCLUDE AND APPLY

1. **COMMUNICATE** Describe all the stages of mealworm development.

2. **DRAW CONCLUSIONS** Use your drawings to arrange the stages in the order in which you think mealworm development occurs.

GOING FURTHER: Apply

3. **COMPARE** How does the way a mealworm grows and changes differ from other animals like cats and dogs?

How Do Mealworms Change as They Grow?

Most young animals look like smaller copies of their parents. Puppies look like small dogs. Chicks look like small birds. They grow larger as they grow older. As the Explore Activity showed, other young animals don't look like their parents at all.

Certain animals, like mealworms, go through changes during their development. This process is called **metamorphosis** (met′ə môr′fə sis), meaning "a change in body form." There are two types of metamorphosis—complete and incomplete. Insects such as mealworms and butterflies go through complete metamorphosis.

COMPLETE METAMORPHOSIS

1 Egg Stage
An adult mealworm is known as a grain beetle. After mating a female grain beetle lays eggs.

2 Larva Stage
A wormlike *larva* (lär′və) hatches from each egg. A larva is a young organism with a form different from its parents. After hatching a larva begins to eat.

3 Pupa Stage
When the larva reaches a certain stage, it becomes a *pupa* (pū′pə). A pupa is a stage where many changes take place. Adult tissues and organs form.

4 Adult Stage
When the adult is fully formed, it comes into the world. An adult grain beetle is completely unlike its larva. It has a smooth body, wings, and six legs.

Why Metamorphosis?

Metamorphosis allows animals to specialize. Larvae and nymphs specialize in eating and growing. Adult animals specialize in breeding. They come to a new environment where their eggs have a better chance of surviving.

Insects such as grasshoppers, termites, and damselflies go through incomplete metamorphosis. Incomplete metamorphosis has three stages.

METAMORPHOSIS

Complete stages	Incomplete stages
1. Egg	1. Egg
2. Larva	2. Nymph
3. Pupa	3. Adult
4. Adult	
Time: several weeks	**Time:** up to 2 years
Who does it: wasps, ants, bees, flies, beetles, fleas, butterflies, moths	**Who does it:** bugs, mayflies, dragonflies, grasshoppers, cockroaches, termites

INCOMPLETE METAMORPHOSIS

3 **Adult Stage**
The damselfly nymph molts several times until it becomes an adult.

2 **Nymph Stage**
The young damselfly, called a *nymph* (nimf), hatches from an egg. A nymph is a young insect that looks like an adult. The damselfly nymph lives in water and has gills. The nymph keeps growing and changing. After many weeks the damselfly nymph comes out of the water. Soon the nymph sheds its skin, or molts. Small wings appear.

1 **Egg Stage**
A female damselfly lays her eggs on a reed underwater. After some time the eggs hatch.

READING DIAGRAMS

WRITE Study both diagrams. Write a paragraph comparing how complete and incomplete metamorphosis are different.

What Are the Stages of an Animal's Life?

The Explore Activity shows how a mealworm changes as it grows into an adult. These stages of growth and change make up an organism's **life cycle** (līf sī'kəl).

Each different organism has its own particular life cycle. However, all organisms follow the same general pattern of birth, growth, reproduction, and death.

Humans have their own life cycle. Stages in the human life cycle are shown below. Each person's life cycle is different. You may go through different stages at very different ages. Even so, all people have a life cycle that follows the same general pattern. At what stage of the human life cycle are you?

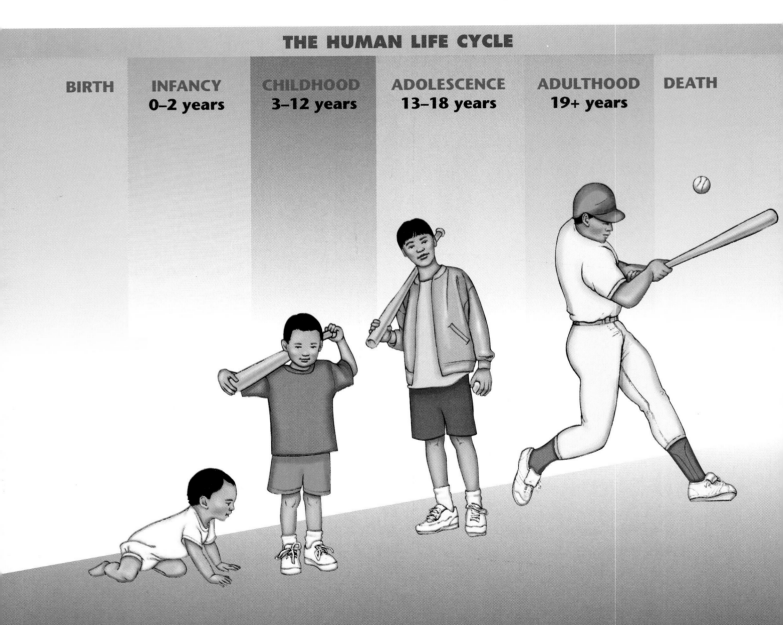

THE HUMAN LIFE CYCLE

| BIRTH | INFANCY 0–2 years | CHILDHOOD 3–12 years | ADOLESCENCE 13–18 years | ADULTHOOD 19+ years | DEATH |

How Long Do Animals Live?

The **life span** (līf span) of an animal tells you how long it can be expected to live. The average life span of a human is about 75 to 80 years. Compare this with life spans of other organisms in the bar graph. Do you see any trends? Do certain animals live longer than others?

Scientists aren't sure what decides an animal's life span. They think cell division may control how long an animal lives.

Throughout an animal's life, its cells divide many times. Scientists think that after many divisions, cells get damaged. Older animals have more damaged cells than younger animals. Therefore, older animals are more likely to develop diseases that weaken them.

What might happen if scientists could slow down cell division? It is possible that animals—including people—could have longer life spans!

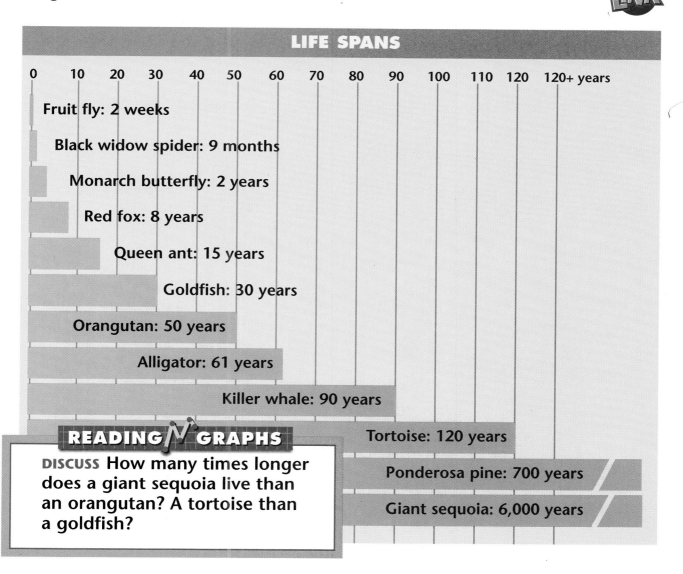

LIFE SPANS

0 10 20 30 40 50 60 70 80 90 100 110 120 120+ years

Fruit fly: 2 weeks

Black widow spider: 9 months

Monarch butterfly: 2 years

Red fox: 8 years

Queen ant: 15 years

Goldfish: 30 years

Orangutan: 50 years

Alligator: 61 years

Killer whale: 90 years

Tortoise: 120 years

Ponderosa pine: 700 years

Giant sequoia: 6,000 years

READING GRAPHS

DISCUSS How many times longer does a giant sequoia live than an orangutan? A tortoise than a goldfish?

How Do Animals Reproduce?

The life cycle of every animal includes reproduction, the making of new animals. There are two types of reproduction. **Asexual reproduction** (ā sek'shü əl rē'prə duk'shən) produces offspring from only one parent. **Sexual reproduction** (sek'shü əl rē'prə duk'shən) requires two parents.

Budding and Regeneration

Simple invertebrates, like sponges and cnidarians, can reproduce by *budding* (bu'ding). A bud forms on the adult's body. It slowly develops into a new animal. After some time the bud breaks off. Each animal then continues its own life cycle.

Regeneration (ri jen'ə rā'shən) is another form of asexual reproduction. A whole animal develops from just a part of the original animal. Sponges and planaria reproduce through regeneration.

Asexual reproduction produces *clones* (klōnz). A clone is an exact copy of its parent. Its traits, or characteristics, are identical to the traits of its parent. For example, a budded hydra is a copy of the original hydra. They both have the exact same traits.

BUDDING

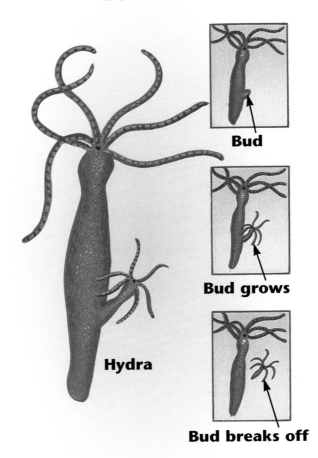

Hydra

Bud

Bud grows

Bud breaks off

REGENERATION

A single planaria is cut in half. Each half grows back its missing part.

Fertilization

Sexual reproduction requires cells from two parents. The female cell is called an *egg*. The male cell is called a *sperm* (spûrm). Their offspring are not clones. They are similar to their parents but not identical. These offspring are new individuals. They have traits from both parents.

Do you think an egg can become a new organism by itself? It cannot. Neither can a sperm. To reproduce, an egg and a sperm must join. This joining is called *fertilization* (fûr′tə lə zā′shən). It produces a developing animal called an *embryo* (em′brē ō′). An embryo can go on to become a new organism, with traits from both parents.

Some animals lay eggs. Egg-laying animals include most invertebrates, reptiles, amphibians, birds, fish, and a very few mammals. In most cases the embryo grows inside a protective shell. The embryo uses stored food in the egg to develop. After maturing the offspring hatches into a newborn animal.

All but a few mammals give birth to live young. One mammal that lays eggs is the platypus.

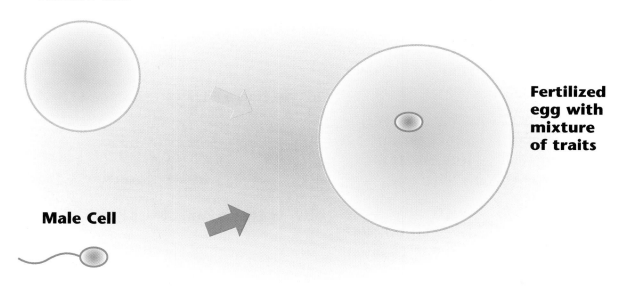

Female Cell

Male Cell

Fertilized egg with mixture of traits

COMPARING ASEXUAL AND SEXUAL REPRODUCTION		
	Asexual	Sexual
Parents	1	2
Male and female	no	yes
Clones	yes	no
Offspring traits	same as parent	mixed
Egg and sperm	no	yes

Heredity Cards

HYPOTHESIZE How many possible offspring can come from six different traits? Write a hypothesis in your *Science Journal.*

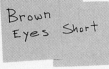

MATERIALS
- pink construction paper
- blue construction paper
- scissors
- marker
- *Science Journal*

PROCEDURES

1. Cut three cards from each paper. Pink cards represent the female, blue cards the male.

2. Write a trait for "Hair," "Eye color," and "Height" on one set of cards. Make sure the traits on the other set are different.

3. COLLECT DATA Match cards to make "offspring." Each offspring needs one card for each trait.

4. REPEAT Continue matching cards to create offspring. Give each a number. Record the traits in a table in your *Science Journal.*

CONCLUDE AND APPLY

1. OBSERVE How many different offspring did you get?

2. PREDICT How many offspring would you get with eight cards?

How Are Traits Passed to Offspring?

The passing of traits from parent to offspring is called **heredity** (hə red'i tē). Offspring inherit traits from both parents.

Each parent has different traits. For example, the mother may have light eyes, while the father's eyes are dark.

When an egg and a sperm join, the traits they carry are mixed like a deck of cards. The offspring ends up with a mixture of traits. Some traits come from the father. Other traits come from the mother.

Female Parent's Traits

■ **Eyes** ■ **Ears** ■ **Nose** ■ **Hair** ■ **Teeth** ■ **Height** ■

╋

Male Parent's Traits

■ **Eyes** ■ **Ears** ■ **Nose** ■ **Hair** ■ **Teeth** ■ **Height** ■

↓

Offspring's Traits

■ **Eyes** ■ **Ears** ■ **Nose** ■ **Hair** ■ **Teeth** ■ **Height** ■

How Can Mammals Be Clones?

In 1997 Scottish scientist Dr. Ian Wilmut got a sheep to produce a clone. The clone, named Dolly, is an exact copy of her mother. Sheep are mammals that reproduce sexually. Never before had a mammal reproduced asexually, and it created a huge sensation around the world. Why do you think his discovery created such a sensation?

How could Dr. Wilmut clone a sheep? He recognized that every cell in the body has special hereditary material. This material contains information for making a sheep.

CLONING A SHEEP

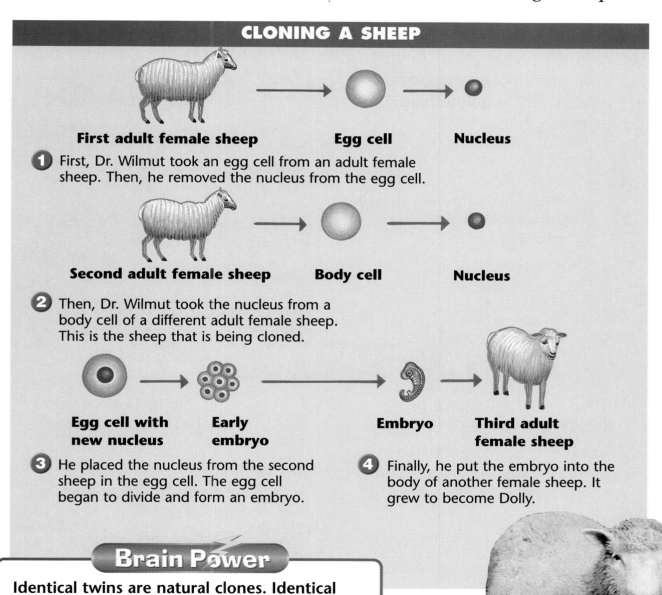

First adult female sheep **Egg cell** **Nucleus**

1 First, Dr. Wilmut took an egg cell from an adult female sheep. Then, he removed the nucleus from the egg cell.

Second adult female sheep **Body cell** **Nucleus**

2 Then, Dr. Wilmut took the nucleus from a body cell of a different adult female sheep. This is the sheep that is being cloned.

Egg cell with new nucleus **Early embryo** **Embryo** **Third adult female sheep**

3 He placed the nucleus from the second sheep in the egg cell. The egg cell began to divide and form an embryo.

4 Finally, he put the embryo into the body of another female sheep. It grew to become Dolly.

Brain Power

Identical twins are natural clones. Identical twins form when a fertilized egg splits in half. Each half goes on to be a complete person. How are identical twins different from Dolly and her mother?

Dolly is the first mammal in the world who never had a father.

Where are you in your life cycle right now? You are probably in the childhood stage. In a few years, you'll reach adolescence, then adulthood. What challenges lie ahead for you? What dangers and opportunities? Knowing about life cycles can help you identify some of the problems that lie ahead and plan for a better future. What plans do you have for your adolescent years? What can you do now to help you achieve your goals?

HEALTH
LINK

ASTRONAUT?
TEACHER?
MOTHER?

What do you think you will become when you are an adult?

REVIEW

1. What is the difference between a life cycle and a life span?

2. What is the difference between complete and incomplete metamorphosis?

3. What is heredity?

4. COMPARE How is sexual reproduction different from asexual reproduction? Give some examples of asexual reproduction.

5. CRITICAL THINKING *Evaluate* Do you think that mammals should be cloned? Why or why not?

WHY IT MATTERS THINK ABOUT IT What would you like to accomplish in your adult years? Why?

WHY IT MATTERS WRITE ABOUT IT Write a plan for how you would like to achieve your goals for your adult years.

READING SKILL Describe the details of how a mammal can be cloned.

The Science of BREEDING

What could you do if you wanted your cows to give really rich milk? Farmers learned long ago that they could choose and mate, or breed, animals with desirable traits. So they bred cattle that produced very rich milk or sheep with longer hair.

How was this done? Let's imagine you have some corn that has many ears on a stalk. You also have corn with very few ears, but those ears are really juicy and full! You want corn with many juicy ears. Here's what you do.

Take pollen from the corn that's juicy and full. Sprinkle it on the flowers of the many-eared plant. Wait until the next harvest, and wow! What a feast!

Of course, this is a simplified version of breeding. It's really a science, and one that's used by farmers everywhere!

DISCUSSION STARTER

1. What animals or foods do you think were bred for specific traits?

2. Why would farmers want to breed animals or plants?

To learn more about breeding, visit **www.mhschool.com/science** and enter the keyword BREEDING.

*inter***NET** CONNECTION

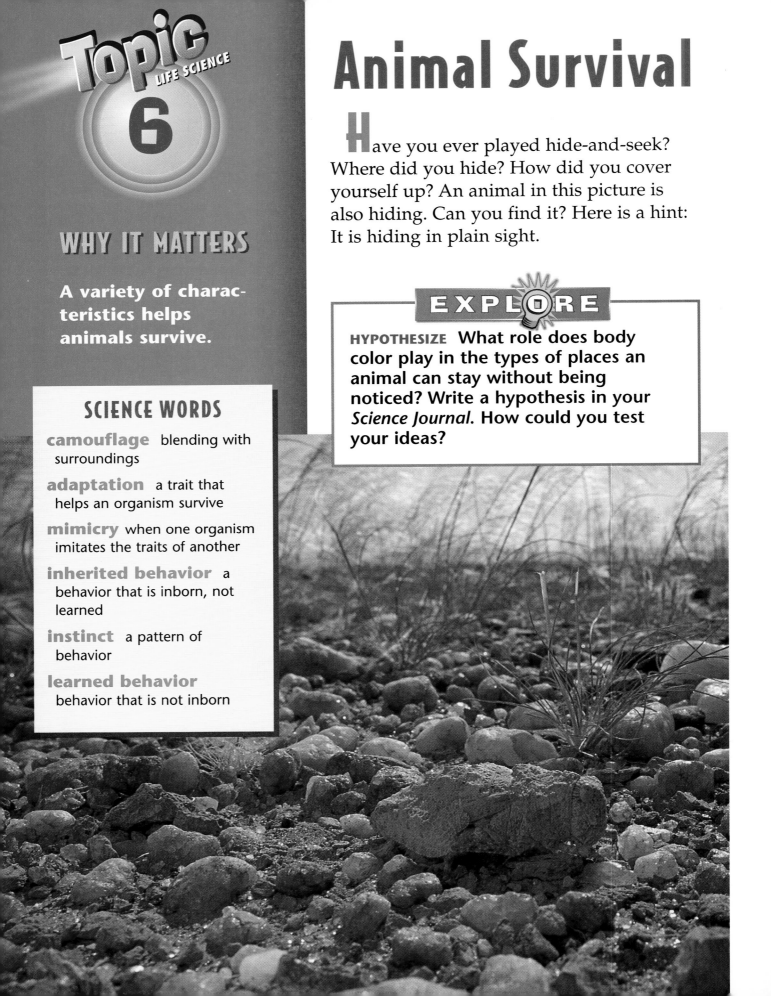

WHY IT MATTERS

A variety of characteristics helps animals survive.

SCIENCE WORDS

camouflage blending with surroundings

adaptation a trait that helps an organism survive

mimicry when one organism imitates the traits of another

inherited behavior a behavior that is inborn, not learned

instinct a pattern of behavior

learned behavior behavior that is not inborn

Animal Survival

Have you ever played hide-and-seek? Where did you hide? How did you cover yourself up? An animal in this picture is also hiding. Can you find it? Here is a hint: It is hiding in plain sight.

EXPLORE

HYPOTHESIZE What role does body color play in the types of places an animal can stay without being noticed? Write a hypothesis in your *Science Journal.* How could you test your ideas?

Investigate How Body Color Can Help an Animal Survive

Test your ideas by pretending to be a bird searching for worms. Which color worms are easiest to see?

MATERIALS

- colored toothpicks
- plastic bag or shoe box
- label or piece of masking tape
- marking pen
- *Science Journal*

PROCEDURES

1. Label your bag or box with your name. This is your "nest." Use it to hold all the toothpick "worms" that you collect.

2. **OBSERVE** Follow the rules given by your teacher to capture the worms. Record the rules in your *Science Journal*. Also record any observations that you make while collecting the worms.

3. **COMMUNICATE** When you are done, record your results in a bar graph like the one shown.

CONCLUDE AND APPLY

1. **EXPLAIN** Which color worms were easiest to see? Why?

2. **EXPLAIN** Which color worms were hardest to see? Why?

3. **DRAW CONCLUSIONS** If you were to become a toothpick worm, what color would you want to be? Why?

GOING FURTHER: Problem Solving

4. **PREDICT** Colors help certain animals blend in with their surroundings. Why do you think some animals have bright colors? How could you find out?

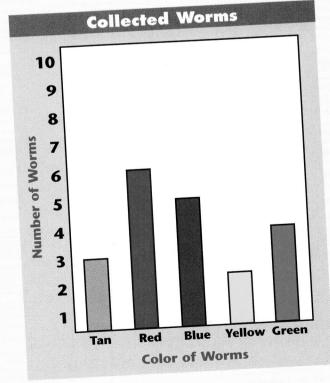

Collected Worms

Number of Worms / Color of Worms

Tan Red Blue Yellow Green

275

Light and dark peppered moths

What do you see in this picture?

How Can Body Color Help an Animal Survive?

The Explore Activity shows how an animal's color can help it blend into its surroundings. Blending because of color is called **camouflage** (kam'ə fläzh').

The peppered moth is a good example of how camouflage helps an animal survive. In the early 1800s, there were two types of peppered moths in England, dark and light. Dark moths were rare. Light moths were common. As a result of increased industry, England's air became polluted in the late 1800s. Suddenly dark moths outnumbered light moths.

Why do you think that happened? Dark moths stood out on light-colored trees. Birds could spot them easily and ate them. However, pollution slowly darkened the trees. The light moths stood out and were eaten.

Why do you think some animals have bright colors? Some display bright colors to attract a mate. Others use bright colors to warn predators not to eat them.

What do you see in the picture above? That isn't a leaf—it's an insect! The insect's body resembles its environment very closely. This is *protective resemblance* (prə tək'tiv ri zem'bləns). The fact that an animal resembles something else protects it.

Camouflage and protective resemblance are examples of **adaptations** (ad'əp tā'shənz). Adaptations are traits that help organisms survive.

What Are Some Other Adaptations?

Body adaptations are called physical adaptations. Physical adaptations help animals survive in their environments. Can you think of physical adaptations other than those listed here? What adaptations do you have?

- **Gills and Fins** They allow fish to breathe and swim underwater.

- **Fur** Thick white fur helps a polar bear blend in with its snowy surroundings. It also keeps the bear warm.

- **Legs** The long legs of the horse help it run at great speed.

- **Neck** A giraffe's long legs and neck allow it to reach leaves high up in trees, where other animals can't reach.

- **Shell** A hard outer shell protects a turtle's soft body parts.

- **Trunk** A trunk helps an elephant grasp things, and feed itself.

- **Eyes and Ears** The keen eyes of an owl help it spot prey from great distances. Sensitive ears allow it to detect prey in the dark.

Do you think that an animal chooses its adaptations? It does not. Adaptations happen naturally. The peppered moths didn't choose to be dark or light. The birds simply ate the light-colored moths because they were easier to see on the dark trees.

For any adaptation survival is the key. An adaptation that helps an animal survive is likely to become more common. Adaptations that do not increase survival are unlikely to become common.

This giraffe can reach leaves high up in trees.

Is That What You Think It Is?

Monarch butterflies have an important adaptation that helps them survive—they don't taste good. Predators spit out monarch butterflies if they eat them. Monarch butterfly bodies contain a poison that they get from feeding on the milkweed plant.

Most predators stay away from monarch butterflies. They recognize the bold, bright coloring. Predators also stay away from the viceroy butterfly. The viceroy is not poisonous, nor does it taste bad. However, it looks very similar to the monarch. Most predators won't take a chance eating it.

The viceroy butterfly is protected by **mimicry** (mim′i krē). Mimicry occurs when one organism imitates another. What advantage does mimicry give animals?

How did the viceroy come to resemble the bad-tasting monarch? At one time there probably was a variety of viceroy butterflies. The ones that looked like monarchs survived. The ones that looked less like monarchs got eaten. As time passed, the viceroys that looked more and more like monarchs survived.

Monarch butterfly

Viceroy butterfly

Skill: Forming a Hypothesis

HOW DO ADAPTATIONS HELP AN ANIMAL SURVIVE?

Every science experiment begins with a hypothesis. A hypothesis is a statement you can test. "Dogs like big bones best" is a hypothesis. You could test this hypothesis by giving dogs different-sized bones.

In this activity you will design two different kinds of animals—a super predator and an animal that is skilled at avoiding predators. Then form a hypothesis about how the adaptations would help each animal in different situations.

MATERIALS

- modeling clay
- construction paper
- drawing materials
- *Science Journal*

PROCEDURES

1. **PLAN** What traits should your predator have? Record them in your *Science Journal*. Describe how these traits would help the animal.

2. **REPEAT** Do the same for your avoider animal.

3. **COMMUNICATE** Make a table like the one shown for each animal. Fill in each category that applies. Add any extra categories that you need.

4. **MAKE A MODEL** Make models or colored drawings of your animals. Label all the features of your animals. Tell how they function.

5. **HYPOTHESIZE** How would these features help the animal survive?

CONCLUDE AND APPLY

1. **COMMUNICATE** What are the animals' most important features? How would they use these features?

2. **EXPLAIN** Review your hypothesis. How could you test it?

3. **PREDICT** Predict what would happen if you could test your hypothesis.

Animal Name_____
Predator ☐   Avoider ☐
Food_____
Enemies_____
Environment_____

Trait	How It Helps
Length	
Weight	
Shape	
Coloring	
Pattern	
Skin	
Arms	
Legs	
Tails	
Fins	
Eyesight	
Hearing	
Smell	
Strength	
Quickness	
Intelligence	

How Do Actions Help Animals Survive?

You learned how physical adaptations help animals survive. Another kind of adaptation involves behaviors, or actions.

One type of behavior is not learned. It is an **inherited behavior** (in her'it əd   bi hāv'yər). The simplest inherited behavior is a *reflex* (rē'fleks'). A reflex is automatic, like scratching an itch.

A spider knows how to spin a web because of instinct.

Complicated inherited behavior is called **instinct** (in'stingkt'). Instincts are patterns of behavior, like spinning a web and building a nest. The behavior is complicated, but automatic. The spider and bird do not think about what to do, they just know.

The dormouse is a true hibernator. It loses up to half its body weight while hibernating.

When salmon swim thousands of miles to mate and lay eggs, they are *migrating* (mī'grāt ing). Migration is an instinct. Animals migrate for three main reasons. First, they avoid cold weather. Second, they find new food supplies. Third, they find a safe place to breed and raise their young.

How do migrating animals find their way? Many birds navigate by the Sun and the stars. Other migrators may use magnetic "compasses" inside their bodies.

Surviving a cold winter is hard. Some animals struggle to find food. Others *hibernate* (hī'bər nāt'), or sleep through the winter. True hibernation is a deep sleep. All body processes slow down. Body temperature can drop to just above freezing. Mice and bats are true hibernators.

Bears and chipmunks go into a less deep sleep. Their body temperatures drop, but their heartbeats remain high. They can wake up in an emergency.

Can Animals Learn Behaviors?

Some animal behaviors are inherited. Others aren't. Behavior that is not inborn is called **learned behavior** (lûrnd bi hāv'yǝr). Animals learn through experience and change their behavior. Learning starts with a need, such as escaping predators, protection, and food. All animals do not learn in the same way.

- **Learning to Ignore** Moving shadows pass over a frog. At first the frog jumps. Later it doesn't. It learned that the shadow is not a threat.

- **Copying** Newborn ducks follow their mother wherever she goes. They copy her to learn to find food.

- **Learning from Experience** At first it takes a rat a long time to get through a maze. It is unsure of where to go. Finally, it reaches the food at the end of the maze. After many trips the rat learns to find its way. The rat learns from experience.

- **Using Two Unrelated Things** A trainer shouts, "Up!" If the dolphin jumps, the trainer gives it a fish. At first the dolphin gets a fish every time it jumps. After a while the dolphin doesn't need the fish. It jumps simply because the trainer shouts, "Up!"

Almost all learning involves some form of trial and error. For example, the rat in the maze uses trial and error to find its way. It makes mistakes but learns from them. After a while it can find its way through the maze.

Trial and Error

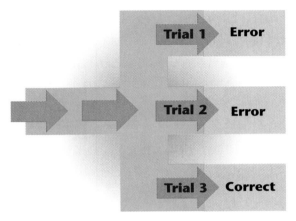

Making mistakes helps you find the correct path.

Dolphin learning also brings together two unrelated things—food and the word *up*. The idea of food causes the dolphin to jump. This is known as cause and effect. The cause is the fish. The effect is the jump. Can you think of any other similar cause-and-effect situations?

Brain Power

Your cat comes running when he hears someone use the electric can opener. Is this an instinct or a learned behavior? Why?

Can Animals Be Trained to Help People?

Can you imagine what it would be like to lose the use of your arms and legs? Quadriplegics (kwod'rə plē'jiks) are people who are paralyzed from the neck down. For them simple everyday tasks can be difficult or impossible. Attendants can help, but they are expensive. Many quadriplegics also like the idea of living on their own.

In the 1970s Dr. M. J. Willard got an idea to use capuchin (kap'yə chin) monkeys to help quadriplegics. These friendly, intelligent animals are perfect for the job. By 1979 Dr. Willard's first monkey was ready to work. It was part of a program called Helping Hands.

Helping Hands trains monkeys, then places them with quadriplegics. First, a baby monkey is placed in a human foster home. The foster family carefully teaches the monkey to perform tasks.

After about five years, the monkey is ready to help quadriplegics. Monkeys are matched with their owners very carefully. For example, an owner who works on a computer is matched with a monkey trained to perform computer tasks.

What do Helping Hands monkeys do? They open books and fetch snacks. They change radio and TV stations. They turn on computers. They perform dozens of other tasks quickly and easily. Monkeys also become companions to their owners and make them more independent. What impact do you think Dr. Willard's program has on the lives of many quadriplegics?

The Helping Hands program needs all the help it can get. It takes a long time and a lot of money— about $25,000—to train a monkey successfully. Do you know of other animals that are trained to help people? Dogs can be trained to help blind people. Some police dogs are even trained to save people!

This monkey helps its owner live a better life. It is a companion and a helper.

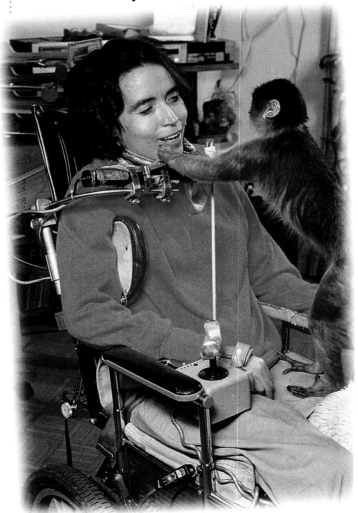

Understanding adaptations helps us learn about ways we can help animals survive. For example, we know that certain animals hibernate. This can make us more aware of not disturbing their resting sites while exploring during the winter. Knowing how animals learn helps us, too. We can train them to help people in need.

It also makes us more aware of our own adaptations—our eyes, nose, ears, and tongue to name a few. Your greatest adaptation of all is your brain. It can produce more learned behavior than any other organism. In fact you are using it right now—to learn!

This dog is a Canine Companion. Similar to a Helping Hands monkey, it is trained to help its owner do many things.

REVIEW

1. How is protective resemblance different from mimicry? How do both help animals survive?

2. Compare and contrast reflexes and instincts.

3. Use "trial and error" and "stimulus and response" to describe how a dog might learn to open the cabinet where his food is kept.

4. HYPOTHESIZE How might having a bright color instead of camouflage help a bird survive?

5. CRITICAL THINKING *Evaluate* A sheepdog is an expert at herding sheep. Do you think this is learned or inherited behavior? Why?

WHY IT MATTERS THINK ABOUT IT
Choose an adaptation you would like to have. What would it be? Why would you choose that adaptation?

WHY IT MATTERS WRITE ABOUT IT
Write a paragraph describing the adaptation you would like to have. How would it help you in your life?

Dancing Bees

If the bee moves up the comb, the food's toward the Sun. If the bee moves down, it's away from the Sun. Moving to the right means it's to the right of the Sun. The closer the food, the faster the bee moves.

The other bees smell the nectar on the dancing bee. They copy its movements, then leave the hive. They fly in wider and wider circles until they find the nectar.

Honeybees dance to tell each other where to find nectar, the sweet juice of a flower. After a bee finds a flower, it fills its honey sac with nectar and returns to the hive.

If the flower is very close by, the bee does a circle dance on the hive's honeycomb. It circles in one direction, then the other. If the nectar's farther away, the bee does a "waggle" dance, moving in a figure-eight across the honeycomb.

DISCUSSION STARTER

1. Why is the bees' dance so important?

2. What would happen if each bee just ate the nectar it found?

To learn more about bees, visit *www.mhschool.com/science* and enter the keyword BEES.

*inter*NET CONNECTION

SCIENCE WORDS

adaptation p. 276
camouflage p. 276
circulatory
   system p. 252
digestive
   system p. 255
excretory
   system p. 254
heredity p. 270
inherited
   behavior p. 280

instinct p. 280
life cycle p. 266
life span p. 267
metamorphosis
   p. 264
mimicry p. 278
muscular
   system p. 256
nervous
   system p. 257

USING SCIENCE WORDS

Number a paper from 1 to 10. Fill in 1 to 5 with words from the list above.

1. The organ system that removes liquid wastes is called the ___?___.

2. The stages of an animal's growth and change are part of its ___?___.

3. Organisms use ___?___ to blend with their surroundings.

4. A pattern of behavior is called a(n) ___?___.

5. All other body systems are controlled by the ___?___.

6–10. **Pick five words from the list above that were not used in 1 to 5, and use each in a sentence.**

UNDERSTANDING SCIENCE IDEAS

11. Describe the processes that must take place for you to catch a ball. Include all the body systems that are involved.

12. Why does sexual reproduction produce more variation in off-spring than asexual reproduction?

USING IDEAS AND SKILLS

13. **READING SKILL: LOCATING DETAILS** Describe some details about organisms to support the idea that learned behavior is not inborn.

14. **HYPOTHESIZE** What causes animals to hibernate? Cold weather? Short days? Low food supply? State a hypothesis that explains why animals hibernate. Then describe an experiment that would test your hypothesis.

15. **THINKING LIKE A SCIENTIST** What advantage would sexual reproduction have in a changing environment? How might it help an animal species survive?

PROBLEMS and PUZZLES

Hot Rhythm By counting the number of times a cricket chirps in one minute, dividing the number of chirps by 7, and adding 4, you can find the air temperature in degrees Celsius. If a cricket chirps 196 times in one minute, what is the air temperature? Will a cricket chirp more or less times if it is colder? If it is warmer?

MATH LINK

SCIENCE WORDS

arthropod p. 227
camouflage p. 276
circulatory
  system p. 252
cold-blooded p. 236
digestive system
  p. 255
echinoderm p. 226
heredity p. 270

learned behavior
  p. 281
life cycle p. 266
mimicry p. 278
mollusk p. 226
sexual
  reproduction
  p. 268
symmetry p. 214
vertebrate p. 214

USING SCIENCE WORDS

Number a paper from 1 to 10. Beside each number write the word or words that best complete the sentence.

1. Fishes and reptiles have backbones and are known as ___?___.

2. Invertebrates with jointed legs and bodies divided into parts are ___?___.

3. Soft-bodied invertebrates that have shells are ___?___.

4. An animal that cannot control its body temperature is ___?___.

5. The system that moves blood though the body is the ___?___.

6. The system that breaks down food for energy is the ___?___.

7. The passing of a trait from parents to offspring is ___?___.

8. An animal with a male and a female parent is the result of ___?___.

9. Bike riding is not done by instinct but is a(n) ___?___.

10. An animal that blends in with its surroundings uses ___?___ for survival.

UNDERSTANDING SCIENCE IDEAS

Write 11 to 15. For each number write the letter for the best answer. You may wish to use the hints provided.

11. Which is not a characteristic of all animals?
    a. They grow and change.
    b. They have backbones.
    c. They need food.
    d. They are made of cells.
    (Hint: Read page 212.)

12. The largest phylum (group) of invertebrates are the
    a. flatworms
    b. sponges
    c. arthropods
    d. cnidarians
    (Hint: Read page 227.)

13. Only warm-blooded animals have
    a. hearts and lungs
    b. backbones
    c. legs and feet
    d. fur or feathers
    (Hint: Read pages 241–242.)

14. The system that carries oxygen to body cells is the
    a. circulatory system
    b. respiratory system
    c. excretory system
    d. digestive system
    (Hint: Read page 253.)

15. Which animals go through metamorphosis?

    a. mealworms

    b. chickens

    c. snakes

    d. all mammals

(Hint: Read page 264.)

USING IDEAS AND SKILLS

16.  **OBSERVE** Give examples of how symmetry is used to help classify animals.

17. What are the major characteristics of flatworms?

18. What are the major characteristics of fish?

THINKING LIKE A SCIENTIST

19. **HYPOTHESIZE** Imagine finding two animals. The animals look different, but they might be similar in some ways. How could you find out if they were in the same phylum? Write a hypothesis to help you decide.

20. Explain what the nervous system does.

WRITING IN YOUR JOURNAL

SCIENCE IN YOUR LIFE

What if people were cold-blooded instead of warm-blooded? How might your life be different?

PRODUCT ADS

Identify the kinds of products or services for animals you might see advertised. What different phyla of animals might they be for?

HOW SCIENTISTS WORK

Give an example from the unit that shows how scientists use classification. Show how and why the classification works.

Design your own Experiment

Do ants change as they grow? Design an experiment to find out. Check with your teacher before doing the experiment.

interNET CONNECTION

For help in reviewing this unit, visit *www.mhschool.com/science*

PROBLEMS and PUZZLES

Identify and Classify

Make a poster that displays information about an animal you find interesting. Explain how you know it is an animal. Classify it as a vertebrate or invertebrate. Does it go through metamorphosis? List any other interesting characteristics. Illustrate your poster.

Market Mimicry

Look for examples of mimicry in store products. Choose a food, clothing, music, or sporting goods store, or some other store. Keep a record of products that seem to mimic one another. Which product is the original? Which do you think is better? Is mimicry a good strategy for store products? Explain.

A Faulty Heart

THE PROBLEM

The Heart-Throb 2000 artificial heart isn't working properly. Blood carrying waste gas is mixed with blood carrying oxygen.

THE PLAN

Study the diagram carefully. Think of a hypothesis that would fix the faulty heart. Your hypothesis should prevent mixed blood from being pumped out of chambers 2 and 4.

TEST

Think of a way that you could test your hypothesis. Show how you could build a model of a four-chambered heart similar to the models in the Topic 4 Explore Activity. Describe how you would test your model.

ANALYZE THE RESULTS

Predict how your model would work. Write a letter to the Heart-Throb company describing how they can fix their faulty hearts. Describe how your heart design might improve the health of their customers.

From body cells

From lungs

To lungs

1

2

3

4

To body

REFERENCE SECTION

DIAGRAM BUILDERS

Building a Frog

All animals carry out the same kinds of life activities. For example, they take in and digest food. **What are the organ systems that carry out these activities like?**

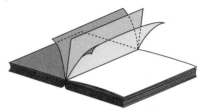

BASE

Explore three systems of a frog. Look at the diagram on the facing page. Lift up all the plastic overlays (1, 2, 3), and look at the page beneath them, the base. You see an outline of a frog.

How would you describe the shape of a frog? How do you think its systems "fit" into the shape?

OVERLAY 1

1 Now drop overlay 1 onto the base. Find the nervous system. **What parts make up this system? In what parts of the body is the system located?**

OVERLAY 2

2 Now drop overlay 2 onto overlay 1. You have added the circulatory system to the diagram. **What parts make up the circulatory system? How does this system "fit" into the shape of the frog?**

OVERLAY 3

3 Now drop overlay 3 onto overlay 2. The digestive system is added. The heart blocks your view a bit. **How does this system "fit" into the animal's shape?**

SUMMARIZE

You can see three different systems of the frog. Do the differences have anything to do with what the systems do? Explain.

DIAGRAM BUILDERS
Activities

1 Make a Table

Set up a table to show the three systems of the frog. You want to show how the systems differ. Decide first on how many columns and rows you will need and what headings you will use.

2 Make a Model

Use modeling clay and art materials to put together a model of the frog with these three systems inside. Share your models with others. What did you do best in your model? How can you improve it?

3 Write an Explanation

How are the nerves arranged in the frog? What other animals have the nerves arranged differently? Why is there a difference?

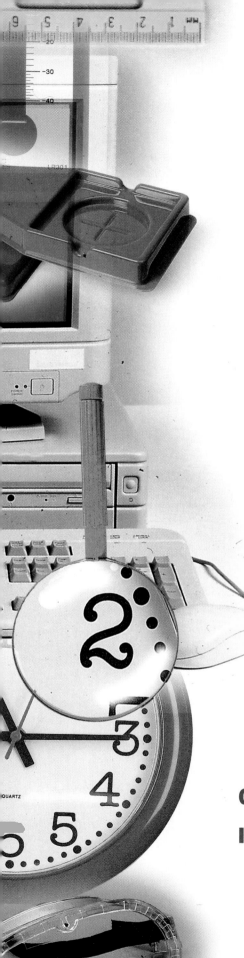

REFERENCE SECTION

HANDBOOK

Temperature

1. The temperature is 77 degrees Fahrenheit.

2. That is the same as 25 degrees Celsius.

3. Water boils at 212 degrees Fahrenheit.

4. Water freezes at 0 degrees Celsius.

Length and Area

1. This classroom is 10 meters wide and 20 meters long.

2. That means the area is 200 square meters.

Mass and Weight

1. That baseball bat weighs 32 ounces.

2. 32 ounces is the same as 2 pounds.

3. The mass of the bat is 907 grams.

Table of Measurements

SI (International System) of Units	English System of Units
Temperature Water freezes at 0 degrees Celsius (°C) and boils at 100°C.	**Temperature** Water freezes at 32 degrees Fahrenheit (°F) and boils at 212°F.
Length and Distance 10 millimeters (mm) = 1 centimeter (cm) 100 centimeters = 1 meter (m) 1,000 meters = 1 kilometer (km)	**Length and Distance** 12 inches (in.) = 1 foot (ft) 3 feet = 1 yard (yd) 5,280 feet = 1 mile (mi)
Volume 1 cubic centimeter (cm³) = 1 milliliter (mL) 1,000 milliliters = 1 liter (L)	**Volume of Fluids** 8 fluid ounces (fl oz) = 1 cup (c) 2 cups = 1 pint (pt) 2 pints = 1 quart (qt) 4 quarts = 1 gallon (gal)
Mass 1,000 milligrams (mg) = 1 gram (g) 1,000 grams = 1 kilogram (kg)	**Weight** 16 ounces (oz) = 1 pound (lb) 2,000 pounds = 1 ton (T)
Area 1 square kilometer (km²) = I km x I km 1 hectare = 10,000 square meters (m²)	**Rate** mph = miles per hour
Rate m/s = meters per second km/h = kilometers per hour	
Force 1 newton (N) = 1 kg x m/s²	

HANDBOOK

In the Classroom

The most important part of doing any experiment is doing it safely. You can be safe by paying attention to your teacher and doing your work carefully. Here are some other ways to stay safe while you do experiments.

Before the Experiment

- Read all of the directions. Make sure you understand them. When you see

  ▨ , be sure to follow the safety rule.
- Listen to your teacher for special safety directions. If you don't understand something, ask for help.
- Wash your hands with soap and water before an activity.

During the Experiment

- Wear safety goggles when your teacher tells you to wear them and whenever you see 🥽 . Wear goggles when working with something that can fly into your eyes.
- Wear splash-proof goggles when working with liquids.
- Wear a safety apron if you work with anything messy or anything that might spill.

- If you spill something, wipe it up right away or ask your teacher for help.
- Tell your teacher if something breaks. If glass breaks do not clean it up yourself.
- Keep your hair and clothes away from open flames. Tie back long hair and roll up long sleeves.

- Be careful around a hot plate. Know when it is on and when it is off. Remember that the plate stays hot for a few minutes after you turn it off.
- Keep your hands dry around electrical equipment.
- Don't eat or drink anything during the experiment.

After the Experiment

- Put equipment back the way your teacher tells you.
- Dispose of things the way your teacher tells you.
- Clean up your work area and wash your hands with soap and water.

In the Field

- Always be accompanied by a trusted adult—like your teacher or a parent or guardian.
- Never touch animals or plants without the adult's approval. The animal might bite. The plant might be poison ivy or another dangerous plant.

Responsibility

Acting safely is one way to be responsible. You can also be responsible by treating animals, the environment, and each other with respect in the class and in the field.

Treat Living Things with Respect

- If you have animals in the classroom, keep their homes clean. Change the water in fish tanks and clean out cages.
- Feed classroom animals the right amounts of food.

- Give your classroom animals enough space.
- When you observe animals, don't hurt them or disturb their homes.
- Find a way to care for animals while school is on vacation.

Treat the Environment with Respect

- Do not pick flowers.
- Do not litter, including gum and food.
- If you see litter, ask your teacher if you can pick it up.

- Recycle materials used in experiments. Ask your teacher what materials can be recycled instead of thrown away. These might include plastics, aluminum, and newspapers.

Treat Each Other with Respect

- Use materials carefully around others so that people don't get hurt or get stains on their clothes.
- Be careful not to bump people when they are doing experiments. Do not disturb or damage their experiments.
- If you see that people are having trouble with an experiment, help them.

Use a Hand Lens

You use a hand lens to magnify an object, or make the object look larger. With a hand lens, you can see details that would be hard to see without the hand lens.

Magnify a Piece of Cereal

1. Place a piece of your favorite cereal on a flat surface. Look at the cereal carefully. Draw a picture of it.
2. Hold the hand lens so that it is just above the cereal. Look through the lens, and slowly move it away from the cereal. The cereal will look larger.
3. Keep moving the hand lens until the cereal begins to look blurry. Then move the lens a little closer to the cereal until you can see it clearly.
4. Draw a picture of the cereal as you see it through the hand lens. Fill in details that you did not see before.
5. Repeat this activity using objects you are studying in science. It might be a rock, some soil, a flower, a seed, or something else.

Use a Microscope

Hand lenses make objects look several times larger. A microscope, however, can magnify an object to look hundreds of times larger.

Examine Salt Grains

1. Place the microscope on a flat surface. Always carry a microscope with both hands. Hold the arm with one hand, and put your other hand beneath the base.
2. Look at the drawing to learn the different parts of the microscope.
3. Move the mirror so that it reflects light up toward the stage. Never point the mirror directly at the Sun or a bright light. Bright light can cause permanent eye damage.
4. Place a few grains of salt on the slide. Put the slide under the stage clips on the stage. Be sure that the salt grains are over the hole in the stage.
5. Look through the eyepiece. Turn the focusing knob slowly until the salt grains come into focus.
6. Draw what the grains look like through the microscope.
7. Look at other objects through the microscope. Try a piece of leaf, a strand of human hair, or a pencil mark.
8. Draw what each object looks like through the microscope. Do any of the objects look alike? If so, how? Are any of the objects alive? How do you know?

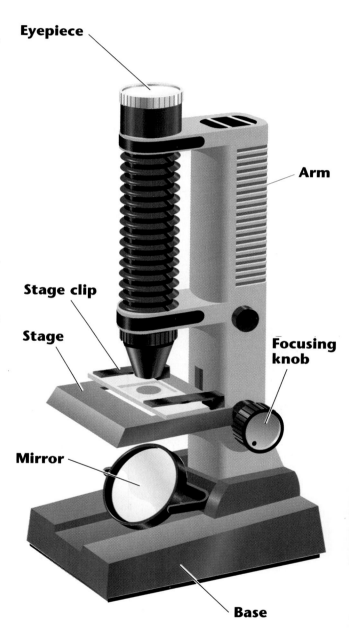

Eyepiece

Arm

Stage clip

Stage

Focusing knob

Mirror

Base

HANDBOOK

Use a Compass

You use a compass to find directions. A compass is a small, thin magnet that swings freely, like a spinner in a board game. One end of the magnet always points north. This end is the magnet's north pole. How does a compass work?

1. Place the compass on a surface that has no magnetic material such as steel. A wooden table or a sidewalk works well.
2. Find the magnet's north pole. The north pole is marked in some way, usually with a color or an arrowhead.
3. Notice the letters *N, E, S,* and *W* on the compass. These letters stand for the directions north, east, south, and west. When the magnet stops swinging, turn the compass so that the *N* lines up with the north pole of the magnet.
4. Face to the north. Then face to the east, to the south, and to the west.
5. Repeat this activity by holding the compass in your hand and then at different places indoors and outdoors.

Use a Compass to Study Shadows

A shadow is the shade that something makes when that thing blocks light. A shadow points away from the light that causes it. Find out how shadows change as the Sun moves across the sky.

1. Go outside on a sunny morning, and look at your shadow. Hold a compass flat in the palm of your hand. In which direction is your shadow pointing? In which direction is the Sun in the sky?
2. Go outside late in the afternoon with the compass. Now in which direction is your shadow pointing? In which direction is the Sun in the sky?

Use a Telescope

Have you ever seen the Moon near the horizon? A little while later, the Moon is higher in the sky. The Moon appears to move across the sky because Earth turns. Do stars appear to move across the sky, too? Make these observations on a clear night to find out.

Look at the Stars

1. Pick out a group of stars that you would be able to find again. The Big Dipper is a good choice. Choose a star in the star group.
2. Notice where the star is located compared to a treetop, a house roof, or some other point on land.
3. Find the same star an hour later. Notice that it appears to have moved in the sky. Predict how far the star will appear to move in another hour. Observe the star in an hour to check your prediction.

A telescope gathers light better than your eyes can. With a telescope you can see stars that you could not see with just your eyes.

The Moon moves around Earth. As a result of this motion, different parts of the Moon are lit by the Sun at different times. The Moon looks like it changes shape. These shapes are the Moon's phases. It takes about 30 days for the Moon to make one trip around Earth and complete all its phases. Check this out for yourself.

Look at the Moon

1. Make a calendar that shows the next 30 days.
2. Each day draw in the Moon's shape in the calendar box for that day. How many days does it take to come back to the same shape?

Use a Camera, Tape Recorder, Map, and Compass

Camera

You can use a camera to record what you observe in nature. Keep these tips in mind.

1. Hold the camera steady. Gently press the button so that you do not jerk the camera.
2. Try to take pictures with the Sun at your back. Then your pictures will be bright and clear.
3. Don't get too close to the subject. Without a special lens, the picture could turn out blurry.
4. Be patient. If you are taking a picture of an animal, you may have to wait for the animal to appear.

Tape Recorder

You can record observations on a tape recorder. This is sometimes better than writing notes because a tape recorder can record your observations at the exact time you are making them. Later you can listen to the tape and write down your observations.

Map and Compass

When you are busy observing nature, it might be easy to get lost. You can use a map of the area and a compass to find your way. Here are some tips.

1. Lightly mark on the map your starting place. It might be the place where the bus parked.
2. Always know where you are on the map compared to your starting place. Watch for landmarks on the map, such as a river, a pond, trails, or buildings.
3. Use the map and compass to find special places to observe, such as a pond. Look at the map to see which direction the place is from you. Hold the compass to see where that direction is.
4. Use your map and compass with a friend.

Length

Find Length with a Ruler

1. Look at this section of a ruler. Each centimeter is divided into 10 millimeters. How long is the paper clip?
2. The length of the paper clip is 3 centimeters plus 2 millimeters. You can write this length as 3.2 centimeters.
3. Place the ruler on your desk. Lay a pencil against the ruler so that one end of the pencil lines up with the left edge of the ruler. Record the length of the pencil.
4. Trade your pencil with a classmate. Measure and record the length of each other's pencils. Compare your answers.

Measuring Area

Area is the amount of surface something covers. To find the area of a rectangle, multiply the rectangle's length by its width. For example, the rectangle here is 3 centimeters long and 2 centimeters wide. Its area is 3 cm x 2 cm = 6 square centimeters. You write the area as 6 cm^2.

1. Find the area of your science book. Measure the book's length to the nearest centimeter. Measure its width.
2. Multiply the book's length by its width. Remember to put the answer in cm^2.

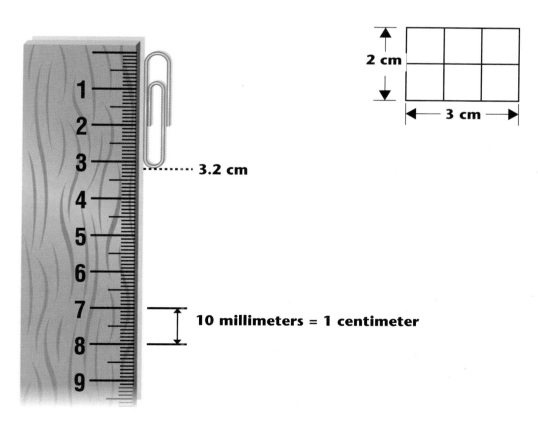

2 cm

3 cm

3.2 cm

10 millimeters = 1 centimeter

Time

You use timing devices to measure how long something takes to happen. Some timing devices you use in science are a clock with a second hand and a stopwatch. Which one is more accurate?

Comparing a Clock and a Stopwatch

1. Look at a clock with a second hand. The second hand is the hand that you can see moving. It measures seconds.
2. Get an egg timer with falling sand or some device like a windup toy that runs down after a certain length of time. When the second hand of the clock points to 12, tell your partner to start the egg timer. Watch the clock while the sand in the egg timer is falling.
3. When the sand stops falling, count how many seconds it took. Record this measurement. Repeat the activity, and compare the two measurements.
4. Switch roles with your partner.
5. Look at a stopwatch. Click the button on the top right. This starts the time. Click the button again. This stops the time. Click the button on the top left. This sets the stopwatch back to zero. Notice that the stopwatch tells time in hours, minutes, seconds, and hundredths of a second.
6. Repeat the activity in steps 1–3, but use the stopwatch instead of a clock. Make sure the stopwatch is set to zero. Click the top right button to start timing.

Click the button again when the sand stops falling. Make sure you and your partner time the sand twice.

0 minutes   **25 seconds**   **72 hundredths of a second**

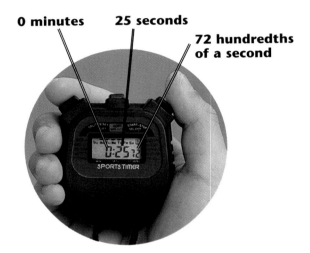

More About Time

1. Use the stopwatch to time how long it takes an ice cube to melt under cold running water. How long does an ice cube take to melt under warm running water?
2. Match each of these times with the action you think took that amount of time.

   a.   **b.**   **c.**

1. A Little League baseball game
2. Saying the Pledge of Allegiance
3. Recess

Volume

Have you ever used a measuring cup? Measuring cups measure the volume of liquids. Volume is the amount of space something takes up. To bake a cake, you might measure the volume of water, vegetable oil, or melted butter. In science you use special measuring cups called beakers and graduated cylinders. These containers are marked in milliliters (mL).

Measure the Volume of a Liquid

1. Look at the beaker and at the graduated cylinder. The beaker has marks for each 25 mL up to 200 mL. The graduated cylinder has marks for each 1 mL up to 100 mL.

2. The surface of the water in the graduated cylinder curves up at the sides. You measure the volume by reading the height of the water at the flat part. What is the volume of water in the graduated cylinder? How much water is in the beaker? They both contain 75 mL of water.

3. Pour 50 mL of water from a pitcher into a graduated cylinder. The water should be at the 50-mL mark on the graduated cylinder. If you go over the mark, pour a little water back into the pitcher.

4. Pour the 50 mL of water into a beaker.

5. Repeat steps 3 and 4 using 30 mL, 45 mL, and 25 mL of water.

6. Measure the volume of water you have in the beaker. Do you have about the same amount of water as your classmates?

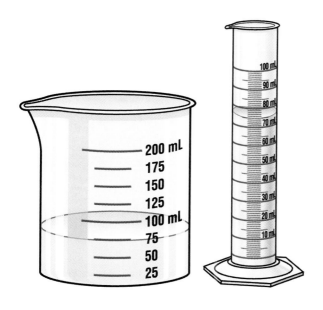

Mass

Mass is the amount of matter an object has. You use a balance to measure mass. To find the mass of an object, you balance it with objects whose masses you know. Let's find the mass of a box of crayons.

Measure the Mass of a Box of Crayons

1. Place the balance on a flat, level surface. Check that the two pans are empty and clean.
2. Make sure the empty pans are balanced with each other. The pointer should point to the middle mark. If it does not, move the slider a little to the right or left to balance the pans.

3. Gently place a box of crayons on the left pan. This pan will drop lower.
4. Add masses to the right pan until the pans are balanced.
5. Add the numbers on the masses that are in the right pan. The total is the mass of the box of crayons, in grams. Record this number. After the number, write a *g* for "grams."

Predict the Mass of More Crayons

1. Leave the box of crayons and the masses on the balance.
2. Get two more crayons. If you put them in the pan with the box of crayons, what do you think the mass of all the crayons will be? Write down what you predict the total mass will be.
3. Check your prediction. Gently place the two crayons in the left pan. Add masses to the right pan until the pans are balanced.
4. Add the numbers on the masses as you did before. Record this number. How close is it to your prediction?

More About Mass

What was the mass of all your crayons? It was probably less than 100 grams. What would happen if you replaced the crayons with a pineapple? You may not have enough masses to balance the pineapple. It has a mass of about 1,000 grams. That's the same as 1 kilogram because *kilo* means "1,000."

1. How many kilograms do all these masses add up to?

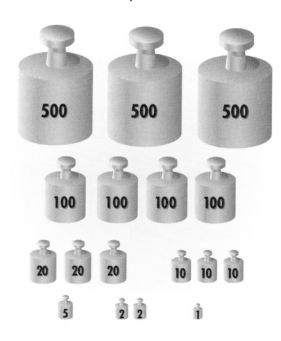

2. Which of these objects have a mass greater than 1 kilogram?
   a. large dog
   b. robin
   c. desktop computer
   d. calculator
   e. whole watermelon

Weight/Force

You use a spring scale to measure weight. An object has weight because the force of gravity pulls down on the object. Therefore, weight is a force. Like all forces weight is measured in newtons (N).

Measure the Weight of an Object

1. Look at your spring scale to see how many newtons it measures. See how the measurements are divided. The spring scale shown here measures up to 10 N. It has a mark for every 1 N.

2. Hold the spring scale by the top loop. Put the object to be measured on the bottom hook. If the object will not stay on the hook, place it in a net bag. Then hang the bag from the hook.

3. Let go of the object slowly. It will pull down on a spring inside the scale. The spring is connected to a pointer. The pointer on the spring scale shown here is a small arrow.

4. Wait for the pointer to stop moving. Read the number of newtons next to the pointer. This is the object's weight. The mug in the picture weighs 3 N.

More About Spring Scales

You probably weigh yourself by standing on a bathroom scale. This is a spring scale. The force of your body stretches a spring inside the scale. The dial on the scale is probably marked in pounds—the English unit of weight. One pound is equal to about 4.5 newtons.

Here are some spring scales you may have seen.

Temperature

Temperature is how hot or cold something is. You use a thermometer to measure temperature. A thermometer is made of a thin tube with colored liquid inside. When the liquid gets warmer, it expands and moves up the tube. When the liquid gets cooler, it contracts and moves down the tube. You may have seen most temperatures measured in degrees Fahrenheit (°F). Scientists measure temperature in degrees Celsius (°C).

Read a Thermometer

1. Look at the thermometer shown here. It has two scales—a Fahrenheit scale and a Celsius scale. Every 20 degrees on each scale has a number.
2. What is the temperature shown on the thermometer? At what temperature does water freeze? Give your answers in °F and in °C.

How Is Temperature Measured?

1. Fill a large beaker about one-half full of cool water. Find the temperature of the water by holding a thermometer in the water. Do not let the bulb at the bottom of the thermometer touch the sides or bottom of the beaker.
2. Keep the thermometer in the water until the liquid in the tube stops moving—about a minute. Read and record the temperature on the Celsius scale.
3. Fill another large beaker one-half full of warm water from a faucet. Be careful not to burn yourself by using hot water.
4. Find and record the temperature of the warm water just as you did in steps 1 and 2.

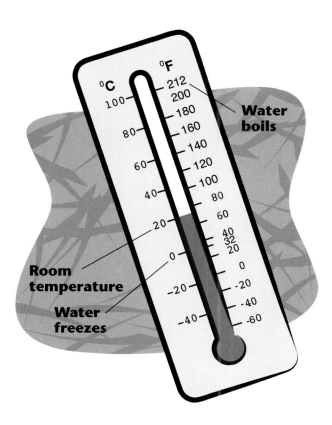

Weather

What was the weather like yesterday? What is it like today? The weather changes from day to day. You can observe different parts of the weather to find out how it changes.

Measure Temperature

1. Use a thermometer to find the air temperature outside. Look at page R17 to review thermometers.
2. Hold a thermometer outside for two minutes. Then read and record the temperature.
3. Take the temperature at the same time each day for a week. Record it in a chart.

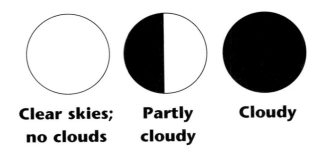

Clear skies; no clouds   Partly cloudy   Cloudy

Observe Wind Speed and Direction

1. Observe how the wind is affecting things around you. Look at a flag or the branches of a tree. How hard is the wind blowing the flag or branches? Observe for about five minutes. Write down your observations.
2. Hold a compass to see which direction the wind is coming from. Write down this direction.
3. Observe the wind each day for a week. Record your observations in your chart.

Observe Clouds, Rain, and Snow

1. Observe how much of the sky is covered by clouds. Use these symbols to record the cloud cover in your chart each day.

2. Record in your chart if it is raining or snowing.
3. At the end of the week, how has the weather changed from day to day?

MONDAY	TUESDAY	WEDNESDAY
25°C Strong winds from south ● Rain	23°C Light wind	

Systems

What do a toy car, a tomato plant, and a yo-yo have in common? They are all systems. A system is a set of parts that work together to form a whole. Look at the three systems below. Think of how each part helps the system work.

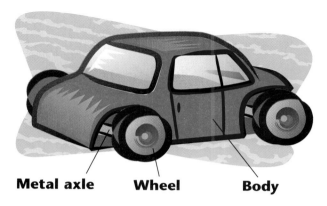

Metal axle   **Wheel**   **Body**

This system has three main parts—the body, the axles, and the wheels. Would the system work well if the axles could not turn?

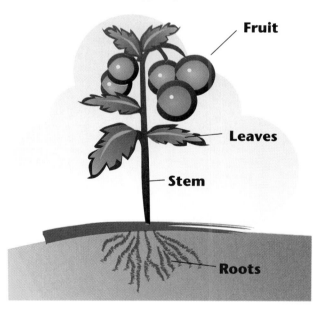

Fruit

Leaves

Stem

Roots

In this system roots take in water, and leaves make food. The stem carries water and food to different parts of the plant. What would happen if you cut off all the leaves?

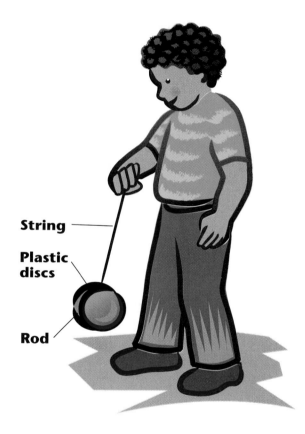

String

Plastic discs

Rod

Even simple things can be systems. How do all the parts of the yo-yo work together to make the toy go up and down?

Look for some other systems at school, at home, and outside. Remember to look for things that are made of parts. List the parts. Then describe how you think each part helps the system work.

HANDBOOK

Make Graphs to Organize Data

When you do an experiment in science, you collect information. To find out what your information means, you can organize it into graphs. There are many kinds of graphs.

Bar Graphs

A bar graph uses bars to show information. For example, suppose you are growing a plant. Every week you measure how high the plant has grown. Here is what you find.

Week	Height (cm)
1	1
2	3
3	6
4	10
5	17
6	20
7	22
8	23

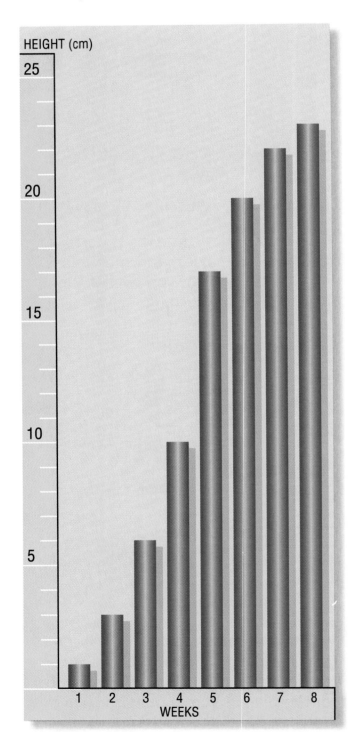

The bar graph at right organizes the measurements you collected so that you can easily compare them.

1. Look at the bar for week 2. Put your finger at the top of the bar. Move your finger straight over to the left to find how many centimeters the plant grew by the end of week 2.
2. Between which two weeks did the plant grow most?
3. When did plant growth begin to level off?

Pictographs

A pictograph uses symbols, or pictures, to show information. What if you collect information about how much water your family uses each day? Here is what you find.

Activity	Water Used Each Day (L)
Drinking	10
Showering	180
Bathing	240
Brushing teeth	80
Washing dishes	140
Washing hands	30
Washing clothes	280
Flushing toilet	90

You can organize this information into the pictograph shown here. The pictograph has to explain what the symbol on the graph means. In this case each bottle means 20 liters of water. A half bottle means half of 20, or 10 liters of water.

1. Which activity uses the most water?
2. Which activity uses the least water?

Line Graphs

A line graph shows information by connecting dots plotted on the graph.

It shows change over time. For example, what if you measure the temperature out of doors every hour starting at 6 A.M.? Here is what you find.

Time	Temperature (°C)
6 A.M.	10
7 A.M.	12
8 A.M.	14
9 A.M.	16
10 A.M.	18
11 A.M.	20

You can organize this information into a line graph. Follow these steps.

1. Make a scale along the bottom and side of the graph. The scales should include all the numbers in the chart. Label the scales.
2. Plot points on the graph. For example, place your finger at the "6 A.M." on the bottom line. Place a finger from your other hand on the "10" on the left line. Move your "6 A.M." finger up and your "10" finger to the right until they meet, and make a pencil point. Plot the other points in this way.
3. Connect the points with a line.

A Family's Daily Use of Water

Make Maps to Show Information

HANDBOOK

Locate Places

A map is a drawing that shows an area from above. Most maps have numbers and letters along the top and side. They help you find places easily. For example, what if you wanted to find the library on the map below. It is located at D7. Place a finger on the letter D along the side of the map and another finger on the number 7 at the top. Then move your fingers straight across and down the map until they meet. The library is located where D and 7 meet, or very nearby.

1. What building is located at G3?
2. The hospital is located three blocks south and three blocks east of the library. What is its number and letter?
3. Make a map of an area in your community. It might be a park or the area between your home and school. Include numbers and letters along the top and side. Use a compass to find north, and mark north on your map. Exchange maps with classmates.

Idea Maps

The map below left shows how places are connected to each other. Idea maps, on the other hand, show how ideas are connected to each other. Idea maps help you organize information about a topic.

Look at the idea map below. It connects ideas about water. This map shows that Earth's water is either fresh water or salt water. The map also shows four sources of fresh water. You can see that there is no connection between "rivers" and "salt water" on the map. This reminds you that salt water does not flow in rivers.

Make an idea map about a topic you are learning in science. Your map can include words, phrases, or even sentences. Arrange your map in a way that makes sense to you and helps you understand the ideas.

North

	1	2	3	4	5	6	7	8	9	10
A										
B										
C										
D						Library				
E										
F		Store								Hospital
G										

West **East**

South

MATH LINK

Make Tables and Charts to Organize Data

Tables help you organize data during experiments. Most tables have columns that run up and down, and rows that run across. The columns and rows have headings that tell you what kind of data goes in each part of the table.

A Sample Table

What if you are going to do an experiment to find out how long different kinds of seeds take to sprout? Before you begin the experiment, you should set up your table. Follow these steps.

1. In this experiment you will plant 20 radish seeds, 20 bean seeds, and 20 corn seeds. Your table must show how many of each kind of seed sprouted on days 1, 2, 3, 4, and 5.
2. Make your table with columns, rows, and headings. You might use a computer. Some computer programs let you build a table with just the click of a mouse. You can delete or add columns and rows if you need to.
3. Give your table a title. Your table could look like the one here.

TYPES OF SEEDS	NUMBER OF SEEDS THAT SPROUT				
	DAY 1	DAY 2	DAY 3	DAY 4	DAY 5
Radish seeds					
Bean seeds					
Corn seeds					

Make a Table

Now what if you are going to do an experiment to find out how temperature affects the sprouting of seeds? You will plant 20 bean seeds in each of two trays. You will keep each tray at a different temperature, as shown below, and observe the trays for seven days. Make a table that you can use for this experiment. You can use the table to record, examine, and evaluate the information of this experiment.

25°C   38°C

Make a Chart

A chart is simply a table with pictures as well as words to label the rows or columns. Make a chart that shows the information of the above experiment.

Computer

A computer has many uses. The Internet connects your computer to many other computers around the world, so you can collect all kinds of information. You can use a computer to show this information and write reports. Best of all you can use a computer to explore, discover, and learn.

You can also get information from CD-ROMs. They are computer disks that can hold large amounts of information. You can fit a whole encyclopedia on one CD-ROM.

Use Computers for a Project

Here is how one group of students uses computers as they work on a weather project.

1. The students use instruments to measure temperature, wind speed, wind direction, and other parts of the weather. They input this information, or data, into the computer. The students keep the data in a table. This helps them compare the data from one day to the next.

2. The teacher finds out that another group of students in a town 200 kilometers to the west is also doing a weather project. The two groups use the Internet to talk to each other and share data. When a storm happens in the town to the west, that group tells the other group that it's coming its way.

email: It's going to storm here. The sky is turning dark gray. The winds are sometimes 65 km per hour from the northwest.

4. Meanwhile some students go to the library to gather more information from a CD-ROM disk. The CD-ROM has an encyclopedia that includes movie clips with sound. The clips give examples of different kinds of storms.

5. The students have kept all their information in a folder called Weather Project. Now they use that information to write a report about the weather. On the computer they can move paragraphs, add words, take out words, put in diagrams, and draw their own weather maps. Then they print the report in color.

3. The students want to find out more. They decide to stay on the Internet and send questions to a local TV weather forecaster. She has a Web site and answers questions from students every day.

6. Use the information on these two pages to plan your own investigation. You can study the weather. Use a computer, Internet, CD-ROM, or any other technological device.

Calculator

Sometimes after you make measurements, you have to multiply or divide your measurements to get other information. A calculator helps you multiply and divide, especially if the numbers have decimal points.

Multiply Decimals

What if you are measuring the width of your classroom? You discover that the floor is covered with tiles and the room is exactly 32 tiles wide. You measure a tile, and it is 22.7 centimeters wide. To find the width of the room, you can multiply 32 by 22.7. You can use your calculator.

1. Make sure the calculator is on. Press the **ON** key.
2. Press **3** and **2**.
3. Press **×**.
4. Press **2**, **2**, **.**, and **7**.
5. Press **=**. Your total should be 726.4. That is how wide the room is in centimeters.

Divide Decimals

Now what if you wanted to find out how many desks placed side by side would be needed to reach across the room? You measure one desk, and it is 60 centimeters wide. To find the number of desks needed, divide 726.4 by 60.

1. Turn the calculator on.
2. Press **7**, **2**, **6**, **.**, and **4**.
3. Press **÷**.
4. Press **6** and **0**.
5. Press **=**. Your total should be about 12.1. This means you can fit 12 desks across the room with a little space left over.

What if the room was 35 tiles wide? How wide would the room be? How many desks would fit across it?

GLOSSARY

This Glossary will help you to pronounce and understand the meanings of the Science Words introduced in this book. The page number at the end of the definition tells where the word appears.

A

abuse (v., ə būz′; n., ə būs′) To use legal drugs in an unsafe way on purpose or to use illegal drugs. (p. 474)

adaptation (ad′əp tā′shən) A special trait that helps an organism survive. (p. 276)

addictive (ə dik′tiv) Causing dependence, or a strong need to have a particular substance. (p. 460)

alcohol (al′kə hôl′) A drug found in beer, wine, liquor, and even some medications. (p. 458)

allergy (al′ər jē) A sensitivity to a substance that can cause a rash, fever, or trouble breathing. (p. 471)

alloy (al′oi) A mixture of two or more metals. (p. 96)

alternating current (ôl′tər nā ting kûr′ənt) Current that flows in a circuit first in one direction, then in the opposite direction. (p. 342)

amber (am′bər) Hardened tree sap, yellow to brown in color, often a source of insect fossils. (p. 164)

amphibian (am fib′ē ən) A cold-blooded vertebrate that spends part of its life in water and part of its life on land. (p. 239)

antibiotic (an′tē bī ot′ik) A type of medicine that kills bacteria or stops them from growing. (p. 470)

area (âr′ē ə) The number of unit squares that fit inside a surface. (p. 81)

arthropod (är′thrə pod′) An invertebrate with jointed legs and a body that is divided into sections. (p. 227)

asexual reproduction (a sek′shü əl rē′prə duk′shən) Producing offspring with only one parent. (p. 268)

atmosphere (at′məs fîr′) Gases that surround Earth. (p. 372)

atom (at′əm) The smallest particle of an element that has all the properties of that element. (p. 88)

B

bacteria (bak tîr′ē ə) pl., sing. **bacterium** (bak tîr′ē əm) One-celled organisms that have cell walls but no nuclei. (p. 19)

balance (bal′əns) An instrument used to measure mass. (p. 70)

biceps (bī′seps) A muscle in the upper arm that bends the arm by contracting. (p. 446)

bilateral symmetry (bī lat′ər əl sim′ə trē) A form of symmetry in which an animal has only two sides, which are mirror images. (p. 215)

bladder (blad′ər) The body structure that stores urine until it is removed from the body. (p. 254)

PRONUNCIATION KEY

a	at	e	end	o	hot	u	up	hw	white	ə	about
ā	ape	ē	me	ō	old	ū	use	ng	song		taken
ä	far	i	it	ô	fork	ü	rule	th	thin		pencil
âr	care	ī	ice	oi	oil	u̇	pull	t̲h̲	this		lemon
		î	pierce	ou	out	ûr	turn	zh	measure		circus

′ = primary accent; shows which syllable takes the main stress, such as **kil** in **kilogram** (kil′ə gram′)
′ = secondary accent; shows which syllables take lighter stresses, such as **gram** in **kilogram**

budding (bud'ing) A form of asexual reproduction in simple invertebrates where a bud forms on the adult's body and slowly develops into a new animal before breaking off. (p. 268)

buoyancy (boi'ən sē) The upward force of a liquid or gas. (p. 69)

C

caffeine (ka fēn') A stimulant found in tea, coffee, and many soft drinks. (p. 472)

camouflage (kam'ə fläzh') An adaptation by which an animal can hide by blending in with its surroundings. (p. 276)

carbon monoxide (kär'bən mon ok'sīd) A poisonous gas given off by burning tobacco. (p. 462)

cardiac muscle (kär'dē ak' mus'əl) The type of muscle that makes up the heart. (p. 448)

carnivore (kär'nə vôr') A consumer that eats only animals. (p. 56)

cartilage (kär'tə lij) A flexible tissue that covers the ends of some bones; found in the nose and ears. (p. 439)

cartilaginous (kär'tə laj'ə nəs) Said of a fish with a skeleton made of cartilage. (p. 237)

cast (kast) A fossil formed or shaped within a mold. (p. 163)

cell (sel) The smallest unit of living matter. (p. 5)

cell membrane (sel mem'brān) An animal cell's thin outer covering. It is found beneath the cell wall in plants. (p. 15)

cell wall (sel wôl) A thick, stiff structure that protects and supports a plant cell. (p. 14)

chemical change (kem'i kəl chānj) A change that produces new matter with different properties from the original matter. *See* **physical change**. (p. 104)

chitin (kī'tin) A light but tough material that makes up the exoskeletons of certain invertebrates. (p. 228)

chlorophyll (klôr'ə fil') A material (usually green) found in plant cells that makes food for the plant when sunlight strikes it. (p. 5)

chloroplast (klôr'ə plast') A plant cell's food factory. Chloroplasts contain a substance (usually green) that uses the Sun's energy to make food. (p. 14)

chromosome (krō'mə sōm') One of the threadlike structures inside a cell nucleus that determine an organism's traits. (p. 16)

circuit (sûr'kit) A complete path that electricity can move through. (p. 304)

circuit breaker (sûr'kit brā'kər) A reusable switch that protects circuits from dangerously high currents. (p. 322)

circulatory system (sûr'kyə lə tôr'ē sis'təm) The organ system that moves blood through the body. (p. 252)

class (klas) A smaller group within a phylum, such as all those animals that produce milk for their young. Classes are made up of smaller groups called *orders*. (p. 30)

clone (klōn) An exact copy of its parent formed by asexual reproduction. (p. 268)

closed circuit (klōzd sûr'kit) A clear and complete path that electricity can flow through. (p. 305)

cloud (kloud) Tiny drops of condensed water that gather in the atmosphere. (p. 385)

cnidarian (nī dâr'ē ən) An invertebrate with poison stingers on tentacles. (p. 223)

cocaine (kō kān') An illegal stimulant made from the leaves of the coca plant. (p. 473)

cold-blooded (kōld'blud'id) Said of an animal that cannot control its body temperature. (p. 236)

community (kə mū'ni tē) The living part of an ecosystem. (p. 50)

compound (kom'pound) A substance made when two or more elements are joined and lose their own properties. (p. 94)

compound machine (kom'pound mə shēn') A combination of two or more machines. (p. 139)

condensation (kon'den sā'shən) When water particles change from a gas to a liquid. (p. 385)

conduction (kən duk'shən) The transfer of energy caused by one particle of matter hitting into another. (p. 118)

conductor (kən duk'tər) 1. A material that transfers heat well. (p. 116) 2. Said of a material through which electricity flows easily. (p. 295)

consumer (kən sü'mər) Any organism that eats the food producers make. (p. 54)

continental glacier (kon'tə nen'təl glā'shər) A glacier covering large sections of land in Earth's polar regions. (p. 177)

contract (v., kən trakt') To decrease in size, or shrink, as most matter does when it cools. (p. 120)

convection (kən'vek'shən) The transfer of energy by the flow of liquids or gases, such as water boiling in a pot or warm air rising in a room. (p. 118)

crack (krak) A very harmful form of cocaine. (p. 473)

crust (krust) Solid rock that makes up Earth's outermost layer. (p. 202)

crystal (kris'təl) The clear and shiny particle of frozen water that makes up a snowflake. (p. 390)

current (kûr'ənt) An ocean movement; a large stream of water that flows in the ocean. (p. 396)

current electricity (kûr'ənt i lek tris'i tē) A moving electrical charge. (p. 304)

cytoplasm (sī'tə plaz'əm) A jellylike substance that fills a cell. (p. 15)

D

decomposer (dē'kəm pō'zər) An organism that breaks down wastes and the remains of other organisms. (p. 54)

deep ocean current (dēp ō'shən kûr'ənt) A stream of water that flows more than 200 meters (650 feet) beneath the sea. (p. 396)

density (den'si tē) The amount of matter in a given space. In scientific terms density is the mass per unit of volume. (p. 84)

dependence (di pen'dəns) A strong need or desire for a medicine or drug. (p. 471)

depressant (di pres'ənt) A drug that slows down the activity of the body. (p. 459)

diaphragm (dī'ə fram') A muscle below the lungs. When relaxed the diaphragm pushes up. Air leaves the lungs. When the diaphragm flattens and pulls down, the lungs fill with air. (p. 253)

digestive system (di jes'tiv sis'təm) The organ system that breaks down food for fuel. (p. 255)

direct current (di rekt' kûr'ənt) Current that flows in one direction through a circuit. (p. 342)

discharge (v., dis chärj'; n., dis'chärj) When a buildup of electrical charge empties into something. (p. 295)

drought (drout) A long period of time with little or no precipitation. (p. 412)

drug (drug) A substance other than food that changes the way a person feels, thinks, and acts. (p. 458)

drumlin (drum'lin) An oval mound of glacial till. (p. 177)

PRONUNCIATION KEY

a **at**; ā **ape**; ä **far**; âr **care**; e **end**; ē **me**; i **it**; ī **ice**; îr **pierce**; o **hot**; ō **old**; ô **fork**; oi **oil**; ou **out**; u **up**; ū **use**; ü **rule**; ù **pull**; ûr **turn**; hw **white**; ng **song**; th **thin**; <u>th</u> **this**; zh **measure**; ə **about, taken, pencil, lemon, circus**

dry cell (drī sel) A battery that changes chemical energy into electrical energy. It is made of a carbon rod and a moist chemical paste. (p. 306)

E

earthquake (ûrth'kwāk') Movement or vibration in the rocks that make up Earth's crust. (p. 198)

echinoderm (i kī'nə dûrm') A spiny-skinned invertebrate. (p. 226)

ecology (ē kol'ə jē) The study of how living and nonliving things interact. (p. 50)

ecosystem (ek'ō sis'təm) The living and nonliving things in an environment and all their interactions. (p. 50)

effort force (ef'ərt fôrs) The force applied to a machine. (p. 132)

egg (eg) The female sex cell. (p. 269)

electrical charge (i lek'tri kəl chärj) The positive or negative property of the particles that make up matter. (p. 292)

electricity (i lek tris'i tē) The energy caused by the flow of particles with negative electrical charges. (p. 292)

electrode (i lek'trōd) The negative or positive terminal of a wet cell. (p. 344)

electromagnet (i lek'trō mag'nit) A temporary magnet created when current flows through wire wrapped in coils around an iron bar. (p. 333)

element (el'ə mənt) A substance that is made up of only one type of matter. (p. 90)

embryo (em'brē ō') A developing organism that results from fertilization; an undeveloped animal or plant. (pp. 43, 269)

endoskeleton (en'dō skel'i tən) An internal supporting structure. (p. 226)

energy (en'ər jē) The ability to do work. (p. 129)

energy transformation (en'ər jē trans'fər mā'shən) A change of energy from one form to another. (p. 354)

erosion (i rō'zhən) The wearing away of rocks and rock materials, as when glaciers leave distinctive features on Earth's surface. (p. 155)

erratic (i rat'ik) An isolated boulder left behind by a glacier. (p. 179)

evaporation (i vap'ə rā'shən) The change of a liquid to a gas. (pp. 93, 384)

evolution (ev'ə lü'shən) The change in living things over time. (p. 40)

excretory system (ek'skri tôr'ē sis'təm) The organ system that removes liquid wastes. (p. 254)

exoskeleton (ek'sō skel'i tən) A hard covering that protects the body of certain invertebrates. (p. 227)

expand (ek spand') To swell or get larger, as most matter does when it is heated. (p. 120)

expiration date (ek'spə rā'shən dāt) The date on a medicine label after which the medicine should not be used. (p. 470)

extinct (ek stingkt') Said of an organism no longer alive on Earth. (p. 43)

F

family (fam'ə lē) A smaller group of organisms within a class. Families are made up of still smaller groups of very similar organisms called *genuses*. (p. 30)

fault (fôlt) A break in Earth's outer layer caused by the movement of rocks. (p. 200)

fertilization (fûr'tə lə zā'shən) Occurs during sexual reproduction when an egg and a sperm join. (p. 269)

fertilizer (fûr′tə lī′zər) Chemicals or animal waste used to treat the soil so that plants grow stronger. (p. 423)

filter (fil′tər) A tool used to separate things by size. It works by means of an interwoven material that retains the bigger pieces but allows smaller pieces to fall through the holes of the filter. (p. 93)

filtration (fil trā′shən) The passing of a liquid through materials that remove solid impurities. (p. 424)

fixed pulley (fikst pùl′ē) A pulley that does not increase the effort force needed to move an object but does change the direction of that force. The pulley wheel is attached to one place so that the object moves, not the wheel. *See* **pulley**. (p. 134)

food chain (füd chān) The set of steps in which organisms get the food they need to survive. (p. 48)

food web (füd web) The pattern that shows how food chains are related. (p. 48)

force (fôrs) The push or pull needed to make an object move. (p. 128)

fossil (fos′əl) Any evidence of an organism that lived in the past. (pp. 40, 156)

fracture (frak′chər) A break or crack in a bone. (p. 439)

freeze (frēz) When moving particles in water slow down, lose heat, and change from a liquid to a solid. (p. 387)

fungi (fun′jī) *pl., sing.* **fungus** (fung′gəs) One- or many-celled organisms that lack true roots, stems, and leaves, and absorb food from dead organisms. (p. 19)

fuse (fūz) A device that melts to keep too much electric current from flowing through wires. Once melted a fuse cannot be reused. (p. 322)

G

gas (gas) A form of matter that does not take up a definite amount of space and has no definite shape. (p. 71)

gears (gîrz) Wheels with teeth that transfer motion and force from one source to another. (pp. 138, 358)

generator (jen′ər rā′tər) A device that creates alternating current by spinning an electric coil between the poles of a powerful magnet. (p. 343)

genus (jē′nəs) A group made up of two or more very similar species, like dogs and wolves. (p. 33)

geologist (jē ol′ə jist) A scientist who studies the physical properties of rocks to tell how the rocks may have formed. (p. 148)

gizzard (giz′ərd) A muscular organ in birds that breaks down food by grinding it with stored pebbles. (p. 255)

glacial till (glā′shəl til) An unsorted mixture of rock materials deposited as a glacier melts. (p. 177)

glacier (glā′shər) A large mass of ice and snow that moves over land. (pp. 176, 373)

grounded (ground′əd) Said of an electric charge that flows into the ground, or surface of Earth. (p. 297)

groundwater (ground wô′tər) Water stored in the cracks of underground rocks. (p. 374)

H

habitat (hab′i tat′) The home of an organism. (p. 50)

heat (hēt) The movement of energy from warmer to cooler objects. (p. 116)

PRONUNCIATION KEY

a at; ā ape; ä far; âr care; e end; ē me; i it; ī ice; îr pierce; o hot; ō old; ô fork; oi oil; ou out; u up; ū use; ü rule; ù pull; ûr turn; hw white; ng song; th thin; <u>th</u> this; zh measure; ə about, taken, pencil, lemon, circus

GLOSSARY

herbivore (hər′ bə vôr′) A consumer that eats only plants. (p. 56)

heredity (hə red′i tē) The passing of traits from parent to offspring. (p. 270)

hibernate (hī′bər nāt′) An instinct that causes some animals to sleep through the winter; all body processes slow down, and body temperature can drop to a few degrees above freezing. (p. 280)

horizon (hə rī′zən) A layer of soil differing from the layers above and below it. (p. 187)

humus (hū′məs) Leftover decomposed plant and animal matter in the soil. (p. 186)

I

ice cap (īs kap) A thick sheet of ice covering a large area of land. (p. 373)

igneous rock (ig′nē əs rok) "Fire-made" rock formed from melted rock material. (p. 151)

immovable joint (i mü′və bəl joint) A place where bones fit together too tightly to move. (p. 438)

imprint (n., im′print′) A fossil created by a print or impression. (p. 162)

inclined plane (in klīnd′ plān) A straight, slanted surface that is not moved when it is used. (p. 136)

inherited behavior (in her′i təd bi hāv′yər) A behavior that is inborn, not learned. (p. 280)

inner core (in′ər kôr) A sphere of solid material at Earth's center. (p. 202)

instinct (in′stingkt′) A pattern of behavior that requires no thinking because it is programmed into an animal's brain. (p. 280)

insulator (in′sə lā′tər) 1. A material that does not transfer heat very well. (p. 116) 2. Said of a material through which electricity does not flow easily. (p. 295)

invertebrate (in vûr′tə brit′) An animal without a backbone. (p. 214)

involuntary muscle (in vol′ən ter′ē mus′əl) A muscle that causes movements you cannot control. (p. 449)

irrigation (ir′i gā′shən) A way to get water into the soil by artificial means. (p. 422)

J

joint (joint) A place where two or more bones meet. (p. 438)

K

kidney (kid′nē) One of two main waste-removal organs in vertebrates that filters wastes from the blood. (p. 254)

kilogram (kil′ə gram′) The metric unit used to measure mass. (p. 70)

kingdom (king′dəm) One of the largest groups of organisms into which an organism can be classified. (p. 28)

L

larva (lär′və) A wormlike stage of some organisms that hatches from an egg during complete metamorphosis; a young organism with a form different from its parents. (p. 266)

lava (lä′və) Magma that reaches Earth's surface through volcanoes or cracks. (p. 151)

learned behavior (lûrnd bi hāv′yər) Behavior that is not inborn. (p. 281)

length (lengkth) The number of units that fit along one edge of something. (p. 80)

lever (lev′ər) A simple machine made of a rigid bar on a pivot point. (p. 132)

life cycle (līf sī′kəl) The stages of growth and change of an organism's life. (p. 266)

life span (līf span) How long an organism can be expected to live. (p. 267)

ligament (lig′ə mənt) A tough band of tissue that holds two bones together where they meet. (p. 439)

lightning (līt′ ning) A discharge of static electricity from a cloud to another cloud or to the ground. (p. 296)

liquid (lik′wid) A form of matter that takes up a definite amount of space and has no definite shape. (p. 71)

load (lōd) The object being lifted or moved. (p. 132)

LSD (el es dē) A mind-altering drug. (p. 473)

luster (lus′tər) The way a mineral reflects light. (p. 149)

M

magma (mag′mə) Melted rock material. (p. 151)

magnetic field (mag net′ik fēld) A region of magnetic force around a magnet. (p. 332)

mammal (mam′əl) A warm-blooded vertebrate with hair or fur that feeds milk to its young; most are born live. (p. 242)

mantle (man′təl) The layer of rock lying below the crust. (p. 202)

marijuana (mar′ə wä′nə) An illegal drug made from the crushed leaves, flowers, and seeds of the cannabis plant. (p. 473)

marrow (mar′ō) Soft tissue that fills some bones. (p. 437)

mass (mas) The amount of matter making up an object. (p. 70)

mass extinction (mas ek stingk′shən) The dying out at the same time of many different species. (p. 44)

matter (ma′tər) Anything that takes up space and has properties that you can observe and describe. (p. 68)

melt (melt) When water particles absorb heat energy and change from a solid to a liquid. (p. 387)

metamorphic rock (met′ə môr′fik rok) Rock whose form has been changed by heat and/or pressure. (p. 154)

metamorphosis (met′ə môr′fə sis) A process of changes during certain animals' development. (p. 264)

metric system (met′rik sis′təm) A system of measurement based on units of ten. (p. 80)

microorganism (mī′krō ôr′gə niz′əm) An organism that is so small you need a microscope to see it. (p. 8)

migrate (mī′grāt) An instinct that causes some animals to move to a different area to either avoid cold weather, find new food supplies, or find a safe place to breed and raise their young. (p. 280)

mimicry (mim′i krē) When one organism imitates the traits of another. (p. 278)

mineral (min′ər əl) A naturally occurring substance, neither plant nor animal. (p. 148)

misuse (*v.*, mis ūz′) To use a legal drug improperly or in an unsafe way. (p. 474)

mixture (miks′chər) Two or more types of matter that are mixed together and keep their own properties. (p. 92)

mold (mōld) *n.*, A fossil clearly showing the outside features of the organism. (p. 163)

mollusk (mol′əsk) A soft-bodied invertebrate. (p. 226)

molting (mōl′ting) A process by which an arthropod sheds its exoskeleton. (p. 228)

moraine (mə rān′) Rock debris carried and deposited as a glacier melts. (p. 177)

PRONUNCIATION KEY

a **at**; ā **ape**; ä **far**; âr **care**; e **end**; ē **me**; i **it**; ī **ice**; îr **pierce**; o **hot**; ō **old**; ô **fork**; oi **oil**; ou **out**; u **up**; ū **use**; ü **rule**; ù **pull**; ûr **turn**; hw **white**; ng **song**; th **thin**; <u>th</u> **this**; zh **measure**; ə **about, taken, pencil, lemon, circus**

movable joint (mü'və bəl joint) A place where bones meet and can move easily. (p. 438)

movable pulley (mü'və bəl púl'ē) A pulley that increases the effort force needed to move an object. The pulley wheel can change position, but the direction of the force remains unchanged. *See* **pulley**. (p. 134)

muscular system (mus'kyə lər sis'təm) The organ system made up of muscles that move bones. (pp. 256, 449)

N

narcotic (när kot'ik) A type of medicine that is used as a painkiller. (p. 473)

nervous system (nûr'vəs sis'təm) The organ system that controls all other body systems. (p. 257)

newton (nü'tən) A metric unit for weight, measuring the amount of pull or push a force such as gravity produces between two masses. (p. 83)

nicotine (nik'ə tēn') A poisonous, oily substance found in tobacco. (p. 462)

nucleus (nü'klē əs) A cell's central control station. (p. 15)

nymph (nimf) A stage of some organisms that hatch from an egg during incomplete metamorphosis; a nymph is a young insect that looks like an adult. (p. 267)

O

omnivore (om' nə vôr') A consumer that eats both animals and plants (p. 56)

open circuit (ō'pən sûr'kit) A broken or incomplete path that electricity cannot flow through. (p. 305)

order (ôr'dər) A smaller group within a class. Orders are made up of still smaller groups of similar organisms called *families*. (p. 30)

organ (ôr'gən) A group of tissues that work together to do a certain job. (p. 6)

organ system (ôr'gən sis'təm) A group of organs that work together to carry on life functions. (p. 6)

organism (ôr'gə niz'əm) A living thing that carries out five basic life functions on its own. (p. 4)

outer core (ou'tər kôr) A liquid layer of Earth lying below the mantle. (p. 202)

outwash plain (out'wôsh plān) Gravel, sand, and clay carried from glaciers by melting water and streams. (p. 179)

over-the-counter (ō'vər thə koun'tər) Said of a medicine that can be purchased off the shelves in stores. (p. 470)

oxygen (ok'sə jən) A part of the air that is needed by most organisms to live. (p. 4)

P

parallel circuit (par'ə lel' sûr'kit) A circuit in which each energy-using device is connected to the cell separately. (p. 317)

partly immovable joint (pärt'lē i mü'və bəl joint) A place where bones meet and can move only a little. (p. 438)

passive smoke (pas'iv smōk) Smoke that is inhaled by someone other than the smoker. (p. 463)

penicillin (pen'ə sil'in) A type of antibiotic first developed from a type of mold. (p. 470)

periodic (pîr'ē od'ik) Repeating in a pattern, like the *periodic* table of the elements. (p. 90)

permeability (pûr'mē ə bil'i tē) The rate at which water can pass through a material. Water passes quickly through porous soils with a high permeability. (p. 191)

pesticide (pes'tə sīd') A chemical that kills insects. (p. 423)

petrified (pet′rə fīd′) Said of parts of plants or animals, especially wood and bone, that have been preserved by being "turned to stone." (p. 165)

pharmacist (fär′mə sist) A person trained and licensed to prepare and give out medicines according to a doctor's orders. (p. 470)

phylum (fī′ləm), *pl.* **phyla** (fī′lə) A smaller group into which members of a kingdom are further classified. Members share at least one major characteristic, like having a backbone. (pp. 30, 222)

physical change (fiz′i kəl chānj) A change that begins and ends with the same type of matter. *See* **chemical change**. (p. 107)

plasma (plaz′mə) The liquid part of blood. (p. 252)

pole (pōl) One of two ends of a magnet; where a magnet's pull is strongest. (p. 330)

population (pop′yə lā′shən) One type of organism living in an area. (p. 50)

pore space (pôr spās) Any of the gaps between soil particles, usually filled with water and air. *Porous* soils have large, well-connected pore spaces. (pp. 190, 408)

precipitation (pri sip′i tā′shən) Water in the atmosphere that falls to Earth as rain, snow, hail, or sleet. (p. 386)

prescription (pri skrip′shən) An order from a doctor, usually for medicine. (p. 470)

producer (prə dü′sər) An organism, such as a plant, that makes food. (p. 54)

property (prop′ər tē) A characteristic of something that you can observe, such as mass, volume, weight, and density. (p. 68)

protective resemblance (prə tek′tiv ri zem′bləns) A type of adaptation in which an animal resembles something in its environment. (p. 276)

protist (prō′tist) Any of a variety of one-celled organisms that live in pond water. (p. 19)

pulley (pul′ē) A grooved wheel that turns by the action of a rope in the groove. *See* **fixed pulley** and **movable pulley**. (p. 134)

pupa (pū′pə) A stage of some organisms that follows the larva stage in complete metamorphosis; many changes take place as adult tissues and organs form. (p. 266)

R

radial symmetry (rā′dē əl sim′ə trē) A form of symmetry in which an animal has matching body parts that extend outward from a central point. (p. 215)

radiate (rā′dē āt′) To send energy traveling in all directions through space. (p. 354)

radiation (rā′dē ā′shən) The transfer of heat through space. (p. 119)

rechargeable battery (rē charj′ə bəl bat′ə rē) A battery in which the chemical reactions can be reversed by a recharger, allowing these batteries to be used again and again. (p. 357)

reflex (rē′fleks′) The simplest inherited behavior, which is automatic, like an animal scratching an itch. (p. 280)

regeneration (rē jen′ə rā′shən) A form of asexual reproduction in simple animals in which a whole animal develops from just a part of the original animal. (p. 268)

relative age (rel′ə tiv āj) The age of something compared to the age of another thing. (p. 153)

PRONUNCIATION KEY

a **at**; ā **ape**; ä **far**; âr **care**; e **end**; ē **me**; i **it**; ī **ice**; îr **pierce**; o **hot**; ō **old**; ô **fork**; oi **oil**; ou **out**; u **up**; ū **use**; ü **rule**; u̇ **pull**; ûr **turn**; hw **white**; ng **song**; th **thin**; <u>th</u> **this**; zh **measure**; ə **about, taken, pencil, lemon, circus**

reptile (rep′tǝl) A cold-blooded vertebrate that lives on land and has a backbone, an endoskeleton, and waterproof skin with scales or plates. (p. 240)

resistor (ri zis′tǝr) A material through which electricity has difficulty flowing. (p. 307)

respiratory system (res′pǝr ǝ tôr′ē sis′tǝm) The organ system that brings oxygen to body cells and removes waste gas. (p. 253)

rock cycle (rok sī′kǝl) A never-ending process by which rocks are changed from one type to another. (p. 155)

rock debris (rok dǝ brē′) Boulders, rock fragments, gravel, sand, and soil that are picked up by a glacier as it moves. (p. 176)

runoff (run′ôf′) The water that flows over Earth's surface but does not evaporate or soak into the ground. (p. 409)

S

scale (skāl) An instrument used to measure weight. (p. 83)

screw (skrü) An inclined plane that is wrapped around a pole. (p. 137)

sediment (sed′ǝ mǝnt) Deposited rock particles and other materials that settle in a liquid. (p. 152)

sedimentary rock (sed′ǝ men′tǝ rē rok) Rock formed from bits or layers of rocks cemented together. (p. 152)

seismic wave (sīz′mik wāv) A vibration caused by rocks moving and breaking along faults. (p. 200)

seismogram (sīz′mǝ gram′) The record of seismic waves made by a seismograph. (p. 201)

seismograph (sīz′mǝ graf′) An instrument that detects, measures, and records the energy of earthquake vibrations. (p. 198)

septic tank (sep′tik tangk) An underground tank in which sewage is broken down by bacteria. (p. 425)

series circuit (sîr′ēz sûr′kit) A circuit in which the current must flow through one energy-using device in order to flow through the other. (p. 316)

sewage (sü′ij) Water mixed with waste. (p. 425)

sewer (sü′ǝr) A large pipe or channel that carries sewage to a sewage treatment plant. (p. 425)

sexual reproduction (sek′shü ǝl rē′prǝ duk′shǝn) Producing offspring with two parents. (p. 268)

short circuit (shôrt sûr′kit) When too much current flows through a conductor. (p. 308)

side effect (sīd i fekt′) An unwanted result of using a medicine. (p. 471)

simple machine (sim′pǝl mǝ shēn′) A machine with few moving parts that makes it easier to do work. (p. 130)

skeletal muscle (skel′i tǝl mus′ǝl) A muscle that is attached to a bone and allows movement. (p. 446)

skeletal system (skel′i tǝl sis′tǝm) The organ system made up of bones, cartilage, and ligaments. (pp. 256, 439)

skeleton (skel′i tǝn) An internal supporting frame that gives the body its shape and protects many organs. (p. 436)

smooth muscle (smüth mus′ǝl) The type of muscle that makes up internal organs and blood vessels. (p. 449)

soil profile (soil prō′fïl) A vertical section of soil from the surface down to bedrock. (p. 187)

soil water (soil wô′tǝr) Water that soaks into the ground. (p. 374)

solid (sol′id) A form of matter that has a definite shape and takes up a definite amount of space. (p. 70)

species (spē′shēz) The smallest classification group, made up of only one type of organism that can reproduce with others of the same species; for example, all dogs belong to the same species. (p. 30)

sperm (spûrm) The male sex cell. (p. 269)

spherical symmetry (sfer′i kəl sim′ə trē) A form of symmetry in which the parts of an animal with a round body match up when it is folded through its center. (p. 215)

sponge (spunj) The simplest kind of invertebrate. (p. 214)

sprain (sprān) A pull or tear in a muscle or ligament. (p. 439)

standard unit (stan′dərd ū′nit) A unit of measure that people all understand and agree to use. (p. 80)

state (stāt) A form of matter, such as a solid, liquid, or gas; how quickly the particles of matter vibrate, how much heat energy they have, and how they are arranged determine the state of matter. (p. 70)

static electricity (stat′ik i lek tris′i tē) A buildup of an electrical charge. (p. 294)

stimulant (stim′yə lənt) A substance that speeds up the activity of the body. (p. 462)

streak plate (strēk plāt) A glass plate that a mineral can be rubbed against to find out the color of the streak it leaves. (p. 149)

subsoil (sub′soil′) A hard layer of clay and minerals that lies beneath topsoil. (p. 187)

surface current (sûr′fis kûr′ənt) The movement of the ocean caused by steady winds blowing over the ocean. (p. 397)

switch (swich) A device that can open or close an electric circuit. (p. 309)

symmetry (sim′ə trē) The way an animal's body parts match up around a point or central line. (p. 214)

system (sis′təm) A group of parts that work together. (p. 6)

T

tar (tär) A sticky, brown substance found in tobacco. (p. 462)

temperature (tem′pər ə chər) A measure of how hot or cold something is. (p. 121)

tendon (ten′dən) A strong band of tissue that connects a muscle to bone. (p. 447)

terminal (tûr′mə nəl) One of two places where wires can be attached to a cell or battery. (p. 306)

terminus (tûr′mə nəs) The end, or outer margin, of a glacier where rock debris accumulates. (p. 177)

thermometer (thər mom′i tər) An instrument used to measure temperature. (p. 121)

tide (tīd) The rise and fall of ocean water levels. (p. 398)

tissue (tish′ü) A group of similar cells that work together to carry out a job. (p. 5)

topsoil (top′soil′) The dark, top layer of soil, rich in humus and minerals, in which many tiny organisms live and most plants grow. (p. 187)

trait (trāt) A characteristic of an organism. (p. 28)

tranquilizer (trang′kwə lī′zər) A type of medicine used to calm a person. (p. 472)

PRONUNCIATION KEY

a at; ā ape; ä far; âr care; e end; ē me; i it; ī ice; îr pierce; o hot; ō old; ô fork; oi oil; ou out; u up; ū use; ü rule; ů pull; ûr turn; hw white; ng song; th thin; <u>th</u> this; zh measure; ə about, taken, pencil, lemon, circus

transformer (trans fôr′mər) A device in which alternating current in one coil produces current in a second coil. (p. 346)

transpiration (tran′spə rā′shən) The process whereby plants release water vapor into the air through their leaves. (p. 411)

triceps (trī′seps) A muscle on the outside of the upper arm that straightens the arm by contracting. (p. 446)

U

urine (yùr′in) The concentrated wastes filtered by the kidneys. (p. 254)

V

vacuole (vak′ū ōl′) A holding bin for food, water, and waste. (p. 15)

vertebrate (vûr′tə brāt′) An animal with a backbone. (p. 214)

virus (vī′rəs) Nonliving particles smaller than cells that are able to reproduce inside living cells. (p. 20)

volt (vōlt) A unit for measuring the force that makes negative charges flow. (p. 345)

volume (vol′ūm) How much space an object takes up. (p. 81)

voluntary muscle (vol′ən ter′ē mus′əl) A muscle that causes movements you can control. (p. 449)

W

warm-blooded (wôrm′blud′id) Said of an animal with a constant body temperature. (p. 236)

water conservation (wôtər kon′sər vā′shən) The use of water-saving methods. (p. 426)

water cycle (wô′tər sī′kəl) The continuous movement of water between Earth's surface and the air, changing from liquid to gas to liquid. (p. 388)

water table (wô′tər tā′bəl) The upper area of groundwater. (p. 408)

water treatment plant (wô′tər trēt′mənt plant) A place where water is made clean and pure. (p. 424)

water vapor (wô′tər vā′pər) Water as a gas in Earth's atmosphere. (p. 372)

wave (wāv) An up-and-down movement of water. (p. 399)

weathering (weth′ər ing) The process of breaking down rocks into smaller pieces that create sediment. (p. 155)

wedge (wej) A simple machine made by combining two inclined planes. It translates a downward force into two outward forces in opposite directions. (p. 137)

weight (wāt) The measure of the pull of gravity between an object and Earth. (p. 83)

wet cell (wet sel) A device that produces electricity using two different metal bars placed in an acid solution. (p. 344)

wheel and axle (hwēl and ak′səl) A simple machine made of a handle or axis attached to the center of a wheel. (p. 135)

work (wûrk) To apply a force that makes an object move. An object must move some distance to call what happens work. (p. 128)

INDEX

*Indicates an activity related to this topic.

*Indicates an activity related to this topic.

*Indicates an activity related to this topic.

INDEX

W

CREDITS

Design & Production: Kirchoff/Wohlberg, Inc.

Maps: Geosystems.

Transvision: Stephen Ogilvy (photography); Guy Porfirio (illustration).

Illustrations: Kenneth Batelman: pp. 74, 105, 121; Dan Brown: pp. 376, 384, 385, 388-389, 389, 398, 399, 400, 408, 410; Elizabeth Callen: pp. 284, 368; Barbara Cousins: pp. 252, 253, 254, 255, 256, 257, 266; Steven Cowden: pp. 296, 297, 298, 318-319, 348, 354; Michael DiGiorgio: pp. 56, 58, 215, 222, 236; Jeff Fagan: pp. 132, 133, 137; Howard S. Friedman: p. 54; Colin Hayes: pp. 127, 134, 135, 310, 333, 343, 346, 347, 445, R7, R11, R13, R15, R20-R23; Tom Leonard: pp. 4, 5, 6, 16, 42, 43, 44, 51, 213, 225, 237, 264, 265, 268, 271, 332, 335, 344, 356, 362, 370, 436, 437, 438, 446, 447, 448, 449, 459; Olivia: pp. 24, 61, 64, 100, 141, 172, 205, 248, 285, 294, 326, 365, 404, 429, 454, 477, R2-R4, R9, R10, R13, R16-R19, R23-R25; Sharron O'Neil: pp. 14, 15, 20, 28, 31, 40, 41, 153, 176, 186, 190, 191, 374, 411; Vilma Ortiz-Dillon: pp. 144, 208, 386, 396, 397, 421, 424, 425, 432; Rob Schuster: pp. 84, 108, 117, 118, 120, 179, 307, 322, 342, 355, 358, 359; Matt Straub: pp. 7, 33, 243, 458, 461, 480; Ted Williams: pp. 69, 92, 93, 95, 119, 154, 155, 198, 200, 201, 202, 338-339, 392-393, 456, 457, 463, 465, 469; Craig Zolman: pp. 303, 304, 305, 306, 308, 309, 316, 317, 318, 319, 320, 321, 368.

Photography Credits:

Contents: iii: Jim Battles/Debinsky Photo Associates. iv: inset, Corbis; Richard Price/FPG. v: E.R. Degginger/Bruce Coleman, Inc. vi: R. Williams/Bruce Coleman, Inc. vii: Jim Foster/The Stock Market. viii: Steve Wilkings/The Stock Market. ix: Mehau Kulyk/Science Photo Library.

National Geographic Invitation to Science: S2: t. Michael Nichols/National Geographic; b. Vanne Goodall. S3: t., b. Michael Nichols/National Geographic.

Be a Scientist: S4: bkgrd. Paul S. Howell/Liaison Agency; inset, Stuart Westmorland/Tony Stone Images. S5: David Mager. S6: t. Steven M. Barnett; m. The Granger Collection, New York; b. Corbis. S7: t. Bruce Avera Hunter/National Geographic Society-Image Collection; b. Michael Justice/Liaison. S8: Eric Neurath/Stock, Boston. S10: Robert Halstead-TPI/Masterfile. S11: l. Stuart Westmorland/Tony Stone Images; r. Steinhart Aquarium/Tom McHugh/Photo Researchers, Inc. S12: James Stanfield. S13: l. Tom Tracy/Tony Stone Images; c. Steven M. Barnett; r. Andrew Wood/Photo Researchers, Inc. S14: The Granger Collection, New York. S15: t. National Geographic Society Photographic Laboratory; b. David Mager. S16: t., b. David Doubilet. S17: Jeff Rotman/Tony Stone Images. S19: Stephen Ogilvy.

Unit 1: 1: F.C. Millington/TCL Masterfile; John Lythgoe/TCL Masterfile. 2: Stephen Ogilvy. 3: t., b. Stephen Ogilvy. 7: Stephen Ogilvy. 8: l. David M. Philipps/Photo Researchers, Inc.; r. Astrid & Hanns-Frieder/Photo Researchers, Inc.; b.l. Michael Abbey/Photo Researchers, Inc; b.r. Edward R. Degginger/Bruce Coleman, Inc. 9: Ann & Carl Purcell/Words & Pictures/PNI. 10: l. Enrico Ferorelli; r. Phyllis Picardi/Stock, Boston/PNI. 11: Dan McCoy/Rainbow/PNI. 12: Stephen Ogilvy. 13: Nigel Cattlin/Photo Researchers, Inc. 17: Stephen Ogilvy. 18: l. & r. PhotoDisc; inset t.l. & inset t.r. Biophoto Associates/Photo Researchers, Inc.; inset b.l. Ken Edward/Photo Researchers, Inc.; inset b.r. J.F. Gennaro/Photo Researchers, Inc. 19: t.l. M.I. Walker/Photo Researchers, Inc.; m.l. Biophoto Associates/Photo Researchers, Inc.; b.l. Eric V. Grave/Photo Researchers, Inc.; inset r. CNRI/Science Photo/Photo Researchers, Inc.; r. Joy Spur/Bruce Coleman, Inc. 21: Doctor Dennis Kunkel/Phototake/PNI. 22-23: David Scharf/Peter Arnold, Inc. 23: R. Maisonneuvre/Photo Researchers, Inc.; V.I. LAB E.R.I.C./FPG. 25: Tom & Pat Leeson. 26: Stephen Ogilvy. 27: t.l. Gregory Ochocki/Photo Researchers, Inc.; t.r. J. Foott/Tom Stack & Associates; m.l. Kjell B. Sandved; m.r. Charlie Heidecker/Visuals Unlimited; m.l. Carl R. Sams II/Peter Arnold, Inc.; m.r. Richard Schiell/Animals Animals; b.l. Hans Pfletschinger/Peter Arnold, Inc.; b.r. Mike Bacon/Tom Stack & Associates. 29: M.I. Walker/Photo Researchers, Inc. 30: Margaret Miller/Photo Researchers, Inc. 32: Stephen Ogilvy. 33: PhotoDisc. 34: l. Richard R. Hansen/Photo Researchers, Inc.; r. Jany Sauvanet/Photo Researchers, Inc.; b. Kevin Schafer/Corbis. 35: l. Adam Jones/Photo Researchers, Inc.; m. Stephen Dalton/Photo Researchers, Inc.; r. Scott Camazine/Photo Researchers, Inc. 36: Dieter & Mary Plage/Bruce Coleman, Inc. 37: Edward R.

Degginger/Bruce Coleman, Inc. 38: Francois Gohier/Photo Researchers, Inc. 39: l. Biophoto Associates/Photo Researchers, Inc.; r. Edward R. Degginger/Photo Researchers, Inc. 41: Stephen Ogilvy. 43: Charles E. Mohr/Photo Researchers, Inc. 45: Tom McHugh/Photo Researchers, Inc. 46: Project Lokahi. 46-47: Ken Lucas/Visuals Unlimited. 48: Stephen J. Krasemann/Photo Researchers, Inc. 49: Stephen Ogilvy. 50: Stephen Ogilvy. 51: Stephen Ogilvy. 52: l. Stephen Krasemann/Photo Researchers, Inc.; m. Jim Steinberg/Photo Researchers, Inc.; r. Renee Lynn/Photo Researchers, Inc. 53: b.l. C.K. Lorenz/Photo Researchers, Inc.; m. Leonide Principe/Photo Researchers, Inc.; r. F. Stuart Westmorland/Photo Researchers, Inc. 55: t. Microfield Scientific/Photo Researchers, Inc.; b. Andrew J. Martinez/Photo Researchers, Inc. 56: inset, Charlie Ott/Photo Researchers, Inc. 56-57: Stephen Dalton/Photo Researchers, Inc. 57: r. Stephen Ogilvy. 59: Arthur Tilley/FPG. 60: Chinch Gryniewicz/Ecoscene/Corbis.

Unit 2: 65: Picture Perfect; Phil Degginger/Bruce Coleman, Inc. 66: PhotoDisc. 67: Stephen Ogilvy. 68: Stephen Ogilvy. 70: Stephen Ogilvy. 71: r. PhotoDisc; l. Stephen Ogilvy. 72: r. Charles Gupton/AllStock/PNI; l. Stephen Ogilvy. 73: all Stephen Ogilvy. 74: Stephen Ogilvy. 75: Stephen Ogilvy. 76: l. James A. Sugar/Black Star/PNI; r. Lisa Quinones/Black Star/PNI. 77: James A. Sugar/Black Star/PNI. 78: Stephen Ogilvy. 79: Stephen Ogilvy. 80: PhotoDisc. 82: Stephen Ogilvy. 83: Stephen Ogilvy. 84: Stephen Ogilvy. 85: Craig Tuttle/The Stock Market. 86: Stephen Ogilvy. 87: t. BIPM; b. Stockbyte. 88: PhotoDisc. 89: Stephen Ogilvy. 91: Corbis/Bettmann. 92: Stephen Ogilvy. 94: Stephen Ogilvy. 95: Stephen Ogilvy. 96: PhotoDisc; (soda can) Steven Needham/Envision. 97: Stephen Ogilvy. 98: t. Science Photo Library/Photo Researchers, Inc. 98-99: b. Chris Collins/The Stock Market. 99: Corbis/Bettmann. 101: Stock Imagery, Inc.; E.J. West/Stock Imagery, Inc. 102: l. Jean Higgins/Envision; r. Rafael Macia/Photo Researchers, Inc. 103: Stephen Ogilvy. 104: col 1: l. Michael Keller/FPG; r. Charles Winters/Photo Researchers, Inc.; col 2: t. Ron Rovtar/FPG; b. James L. Amos/Photo Researchers, Inc. 106: l. Stephen Ogilvy; r.t. R.B. Smith/Dembinsky Photo; r.b. Charles Winters/Photo Researchers, Inc. 109: Stephen Ogilvy. 110: col 1: t. Gerald Zanetti/The Stock Market; m. Biophoto Associates/Photo Researchers, Inc.; b. Philip James Corwin/Corbis; col 2: t. Robert Jonathan Kligge/The Stock Market; m. Brownie Harris/The Stock Market; b. Adam Hart-Davis/Photo Researchers, Inc.; 111: Stephen Ogilvy. 112: t. Joel Arrington/Visuals Unlimited; m. David McGlynn/FPG; b. Paul Bierman/Visuals Unlimited. 112-113: PhotoDisc. 113: Sylvan Wittwer/Visuals Unlimited. 114: Richard Ellis/Photo Researchers, Inc. 115: Stephen Ogilvy. 116: Stephen Ogilvy. 117: Stephen Ogilvy. 119: Stephen Ogilvy. 122: t. Edward R. Degginger/Bruce Coleman, Inc.; m. Tim Davis/Photo Researchers, Inc.; b. Hans Reinhard/Bruce Coleman, Inc. 124: PhotoDisc; Ken Karp. 125: Jade Albert/FPG. 126: Debra P. Hershkowitz. 128: l. Idaho Ketchum/The Stock Market; r. Dollarhide Monkmeyer. 129: Hank Morgan/Photo Researchers, Inc. 130: l. Steve Elmore/Bruce Coleman, Inc.; b. Edward R. Degginger/Bruce Coleman, Inc.; r. J. Fennell/Bruce Coleman, Inc. 131: l. Tony Freeman/PhotoEdit; c. Kenneth H. Thomas/Photo Researchers, Inc.; t.r. Tony Freeman/PhotoEdit; b.r. Science VU/Visuals Unlimited. 133: David Mager. 135: Alan Schein/The Stock Market. 136: David Young-Wolff/PhotoEdit. 138: Michal Newman/PhotoEdit. 139: PhotoDisc. 140: l. Culver Pictures, Inc.; m. www.artoday.com.

Unit 3: 145: Carr Clifton; Tom Bean. 146: Sinclair Stammers/Photo Researchers, Inc. 147: Stephen Ogilvy. 148: l.&m.r. Ken Karp; m.l. ©Tom Pantages/Photo Take; r. Stephen Ogilvy; b. Joyce Photographics/Photo Researchers, Inc. 149: t.r. Corbis; t.l. Stephen Ogilvy; b.r. A.J. Copley/VU; b.l. Mark A. Schneider/VU. 150: PhotoDisc. 151: l. Stephen Ogilvy; m.&r. E.R. Degginger/Photo Researchers, Inc. 152: t.l. Charles Winters/Photo Researchers, Inc.; t.r. Ken Karp; b.l. ©Martin G. Miller/VU; b.r. Andrew J. Martinez/Photo Researchers, Inc. 153: Stephen Ogilvy. 154: Corbis. 156: t. J C Carton/Bruce Coleman, Inc.; b. Edward R. Degginger/Bruce Coleman, Inc. 157: Stephen Ogilvy. 158: t. David Burnett/Contract Press Images/PNI; b. E.R. Degginger/Photo Researchers, Inc. 159: NASA. 160: l. Weststock; m. PhotoDisc. 162: Francois Gohier/Photo Researchers, Inc.; 163: l. Charles R. Belinky/Photo Researchers, Inc.; r. Stephen Ogilvy. 164: l. Edward R. Degginger/Bruce Coleman, Inc.; r. Novosti/Photo Researchers, Inc. 165: l. A.J. Copley/Visuals Unlimited; r. Ed Bohon/The Stock Market. 166: Carlos Goldin/Photo Researchers, Inc. 167: A.J. Copley/Visuals Unlimited. 168: l. Tom McHugh/Photo Researchers, Inc.; r. A.J. Copley/Visuals Unlimited. 169: l. Phototake/PNI; r. Phil Degginger/Bruce Coleman, Inc. 170: Richard Lydekker/Linda Hall Library. 171: courtesy Lisa White. 173: N.&M. Freeman/Bruce Coleman, Inc. 174: Lee Foster/Bruce Coleman, Inc. 175: Stephen Ogilvy. 177: Charlie

Heidecker/Visuals Unlimited. 178: Ken Cavanagh. 180: John Serrao/ Photo Researchers, Inc. 181: Joyce Photographics/Photo Researchers, Inc. 182-183: Ron Sanford/The Stock Market. 183: Photo Researchers, Inc. 184: Stephen Ogilvy. 185: Stephen Ogilvy. 187: Black/Bruce Coleman, Inc. 188: Stephen Ogilvy. 188-189: Janis Burger/Bruce Coleman, Inc. 190: Stephen Ogilvy. 192: Kazuyoshi Nomachi/Photo Researchers, Inc. 193: Richard T. Nowitz/Photo Researchers, Inc. 195: t.r. Barry Hennings/Photo Researchers, Inc.; b.l. Franco Sal-Moiragni/The Stock Market; t.l. Gary S. Withey/Bruce Coleman, Inc.; bkgrd. Lynette Cook/Science Photo Library/Photo Researchers, Inc. 196: Stephen Ogilvy. 197: Stephen Ogilvy. 199: l. PhotoDisc; r. Stephen Ogilvy. 203: Russell D. Curtis/Photo Researchers, Inc. 204: Corbis.

Unit 4: 209: Art Wolf/Tony Stone Images. 210: Hans Reinhard/Bruce Coleman, Inc. 211: Stephen Ogilvy. 212: l. Maryann Frazier/Photo Researchers, Inc.; r. Scott Smith/Animals Animals. 214: l. Stephen Ogilvy; r. Charles V. Angelo/Photo Researchers, Inc. 216: t.r. Joe McDonald/Bruce Coleman, Inc.; m.r. James R. McCullagh/Visuals Unlimited; b.l. Neil S. McDaniel/Photo Researchers, Inc.; b.c. Ron & Valerie Taylor/Bruce Coleman, Inc.; b.r. John Chellman/Animals Animals. 217: l. David Doubilet; r. Andrew J. Martinez/Photo Researchers, Inc. 218: Sisse Brimberg/National Geographic Image Collection. 219: t. Fran Coleman/Animals Animals; b. Joel Sartore. 220: l. & r. Chip Clark. 221: t. Kim Taylor/Bruce Coleman, Inc; b. Ray Coleman/Photo Researchers, Inc. 223: inset, Marian Bacon/Animals Animals; t. Sefton/Bruce Coleman, Inc. 224: t. Carol Geake/Animals Animals; b. J.H. Robinson/Photo Researchers, Inc. 226: l. Joyce & Frank Burek/Animals Animals; b.r. Zig Leszcynski/Animals Animals. 227: Doug Sokell/Visuals Unlimited. 228: l. Jane Burton/Bruce Coleman, Inc.; r. Tom McHugh/Photo Researchers, Inc. 229: col 1 L. West/Photo Researchers, Inc.; insets l. & r. Dwight Kuhn; col 2 clockwise from top: L. West/Bruce Coleman, Inc.; John D. Cunningham/Visuals Unlimited; Mary Beth Angelo/Photo Researchers, Inc.; Cabisco/Visuals Unlimited; Fabio Colombini/Animals Animals; Mary Snyderman/Visuals Unlimited. 230-231: L. Newman A./Photo Researchers, Inc. 231: William J. Pohley/Visuals Unlimited. 232: t.l. Richard Hamilton Smith/Dembinsky Photo Assoc. 232-233: PhotoDisc. 233: t. Richard T. Nowitz/Photo Researchers,Inc.; David Young-Wolf/PhotoEdit. 234: Stephen Ogilvy. 235: Norman Owen Tomalin/Bruce Coleman, Inc. 237: Hans Reinhard/Bruce Coleman, Inc. 238: Dave B. Fleetham/Visuals Unlimited; inset, Jane Burton/Bruce Coleman, Inc. 239: t. G.I. Bernard/OSF Animals Animals; b. L. West/Bruce Coleman, Inc. 240: Tom McHugh/Photo Researchers, Inc. 241: Roy David Farris/Visuals Unlimited. 242: Jean Phillipe Varin/Photo Researchers, Inc. 243: clockwise from t.l.: Dan Guravich/Photo Researchers, Inc.; Ron & Valerie Taylor/Bruce Coleman, Inc.; Jeff Lepore/Photo Researchers, Inc.; Dwight R. Kuhn; Wally Eberhart/Visuals Unlimited; Zig Leszczynski/Animals Animals. 244: Stephen Ogilvy. 245: t. Eric & David Hosking/Corbis; b. W. Perry Conway/Corbis. 246: Douglas Faulkner/Photo Researchers, Inc. 247: inset, Kennan Ward/Bruce Coleman, Inc.; bkgrd. Peter B. Kaplan/Photo Researchers, Inc. 249: Charles Krebs/Tony Stone Images; L.L. Rue III/Bruce Coleman, Inc. 250: PhotoDisc. 251: Stephen Ogilvy. 258: Kjell B. Sandved/Photo Researchers, Inc. 259: Stephen Spotte/Photo Researchers, Inc. 260: PhotoDisc. 261: b.r. PhotoDisc; t.l. Larry Cameron/Photo Researchers, Inc.; t.r. Norman Owen Tomalin/Bruce Coleman, Inc. 262: Gerard Lacz/Animals Animals. 263: Stephen Ogilvy. 270: Stephen Ogilvy. 271: AP/Wide World Photos. 272: Stephen Ogilvy. 273: b.r. D. Long/Visuals Unlimited; bkgrd. G. Buttner/Okapia/Photo Researchers, Inc.; r. Wally Eberhart/Visuals Unlimited. 274: Michael Fogden/Bruce Coleman, Inc. 276: Breck P. Kent/Animals Animals; Michael Fogden/Bruce Coleman, Inc. 277: K & K Ammann/Bruce Coleman, Inc. 278: John Shaw/Bruce Coleman, Inc. 280: l. Maria Zorn/Animals Animals; r. W.J.C. Murray/Bruce Coleman, Inc. 282: Rita Nannini/Photo Researchers, Inc. 283: A. Ramey/PhotoEdit. 284: PhotoDisc; b.r. Thomas C. Boyden/Dembinsky Photo Assoc.

Unit 5: 289: PhotoDisc. 290: Tim Davis/Photo Researchers, Inc. 291: Stephen Ogilvy. 292: Stockbyte. 293: PhotoDisc. 294: PhotoDisc. 295: Stephen Ogilvy. 297: Kent Wood/Photo Researchers, Inc. 299: PhotoDisc. 300: l. The Granger Collection, New York; r. Dale Camera Graphics/Phototake/PNI. 301: The Granger Collection, New York. 302: Stephen Ogilvy. 305: Stephen Ogilvy. 309: Norbert Wu. 311: Stephen Ogilvy. 312: b.l. Culver Pictures, Inc.; m. Stock Montage, Inc.; b.r. PhotoDisc; t.r. Rich Treptow/Photo Researchers, Inc. 313: m. Norman Owen Tomalin/Bruce Coleman, Inc.; b.r. Will & Deni McIntyre/Photo Researchers, Inc. 314: PhotoDisc. 315: Stephen Ogilvy. 322: l. PhotoDisc; r. Norman Owen Tomalin/Bruce Coleman, Inc. 323: Stephen Ogilvy. 324: Don Mason/The Stock Market. 324-325: Michael W. Davidson/Photo Researchers, Inc. 325: David Parker/Seagate/Photo Researchers, Inc. 327: PhotoDisc. 328: Stephen Ogilvy. 329: Stephen Ogilvy. 330: Stephen Ogilvy. 331: Stephen Ogilvy. 332: Stephen Ogilvy.

334: l. Stephen Ogilvy; r. David R. Frazier/Photo Researchers, Inc. 336: l. Stephen Ogilvy; r. Science Photo Library/Photo Researchers, Inc. 337: Stephen Ogilvy. 340: AP/Wide World Photos. 341: Stephen Ogilvy. 345: Stephen Ogilvy. 346: Ken Sherman/Bruce Coleman, Inc. 349: Historical Picture Archive/Corbis. 350: Stephen Ogilvy. 351: t. Elena Rooraid/PhotoEdit. b. Dennis Hallinan/FPG. 352: Stephen Ogilvy. 353: Stephen Ogilvy. 355: Stephen Ogilvy. 357: Stephen Ogilvy. 358: Stephen Ogilvy. 359: Stephen Ogilvy. 360: l. Martin Withers/Dembinsky Photo & PhotoDisc; c. Gelfan/Monkmeyer; r. Andrew/Photo Researchers, Inc. 360-361: PhotoDisc. 361: l. Charles D. Winters/Photo Researchers, Inc.; b. Stockbyte; r. Aaron Haupt/Photo Researchers, Inc. 363: Stephen Ogilvy. 364: bkgrd. Arthur Tilley/FPG; b.l. Robert Pettit/Dembinsky Photo; t.r. Schneider Studio/The Stock Market; b.r. Simon Fraser/Photo Researchers, Inc.; t.l. Werner Bertsch/Bruce Coleman, Inc.

Unit 6: 369: Picture Perfect; John Turner/Tony Stone Images. 371: Stephen Ogilvy. 372: Planet Earth Pictures/FPG. 373: l. PhotoDisc; r. Courtesy of Lake Michigan. 374: Roy Morsch/The Stock Market. 375: Joe McDonald/Bruce Coleman, Inc.; inset, Ron & Valerie Taylor. 377: Stephen Ogilvy. 378: Stephen Ogilvy. 379: Wendell Metzen/Bruce Coleman, Inc. 380-381: L.A. Frank, The University of Iowa & NASA/Goddard Space Flight Center; Michael Freeman/Bruce Coleman, Inc./PNI; Chad Ehlers/Photo Network/PNI. 382: Stephen Ogilvy. 383: Stephen Ogilvy. 386: Stephen Ogilvy. 387: inset, Joe DiMaggio/The Stock Market; Lee Rentz/Bruce Coleman, Inc. 390: t. John Shaw/Bruce Coleman, Inc.; b. Howard B. Bluestein/Photo Researchers, Inc. 391: Steve Smith/FPG. 392: Library of Congress/Corbis. 393: l. Barry L. Runk/Grant Heilman; r. Charles D. Winters/Photo Researchers, Inc. 394: Stephen Ogilvy. 395: Stephen Ogilvy. 398: t. & b. Andrew J. Martinez/Photo Researchers, Inc. 399: Stephen Ogilvy. 401: bkgrd. & inset, Courtesy of Bruce M. Richmond/USGS. 402: Wendell Metzen/Bruce Coleman, Inc. 403: bkgrd. PhotoDisc. b. Gary Randall/ FPG; m. Martin Bond/Science Photo Library/Photo Researchers, Inc. 405: Superstock; Chris Vincent/The Stock Market. 406: Culver Pictures, Inc. 407: Stephen Ogilvy. 409: l. Michael S. Renner/Bruce Coleman, Inc.; r. Stephen Ogilvy. 412: l. PhotoDisc; inset, J. Dermid/Bruce Coleman, Inc. 413: Richard & Susan Day/Animals Animals. 414: Stephen Ogilvy. 415: PhotoDisc. 416: l. Corbis/Bettmann; r. AP/Wide World Photos. 416-417: Black/Bruce Coleman, Inc. 417: t.l. AP/Wide World Photos; t.r. Corbis/UPI/Bettman; b. AP/Wide World Photos. 418: PhotoDisc. 419: Stephen Ogilvy. 420: PhotoDisc. 421: Richard Hutchings/Photo Researchers, Inc. 422: all PhotoDisc. 423: b. PhotoDisc; r. Blackstone R. Millbury/Bruce Coleman, Inc. 425: Norman Owen Tomalin/Bruce Coleman, Inc. 426: John Elk III/Bruce Coleman, Inc. 427: Stephen Ogilvy. 428: m. David L. Pearson/Visuals Unlimited; bkgrd. John Shaw/Bruce Coleman; t. John Gerlach/Dembinsky Photo Assoc.

Unit 7: 433: Ken Chernus/FPG; J.Y. Mallet/PhotoEdit. 434: Adam Jones/Dembinsky Photo. 435: Stephen Ogilvy. 439: Stephen Ogilvy. 441: Stephen Ogilvy. 442: l. Billy E. Barnes/PhotoEdit/PNI; r. Dept. of Clinical Radiology, Salisbury District Hospital/SPL/Photo Researchers, Inc. 444: Michael Krasowitz/FPG. 446: Dwight R. Kuhn. 447: l. & c. Stephen Ogilvy; r. Rob Curtis/VIREO. 448: CNRI/Photo Researchers, Inc. 449: Marshall Sklar/Photo Researchers, Inc. 450: Stephen Ogilvy. 451: Stephen Ogilvy. 452: b. Corbis; t. Mark E. Gibson/Dembinsky Photo. 453: t. Blair Seitz/Photo Researchers, Inc.; b. Mark Gibson/Visuals Unlimited. 455: Bill Losh/FPG. 458: Michael A. Keller/The Stock Market. 460: Stephen Ogilvy. 462: Matt Meadows/Peter Arnold, Inc. 463: Arthur Tilley/FPG. 466: PhotoDisc. 467: Mark C. Burnett/ Photo Researchers, Inc. 468: Stephen Ogilvy. 470: José Pelaez/The Stock Market. 473: Bill Beatty/Visuals Unlimited. 474: l. Stephen Ogilvy; r. Jeff Greenberg/PhotoEdit. 476: m. Barros & Barros/The Image Bank; t. Bill Bachmann/Photo Researchers, Inc.; bkgrd. Ed Gallucci/The Stock Market.

Handbook: Steven Ogilvy: pp. R6, R8, R12, R14, R15, R26.